Train Your Your *Money*

Train Your Money
An Expert's Winning Playbook for Your Financial Success

Hillary Seiler

Published by Game Changer Publishing

Paperback ISBN: 978-1-967424-99-3

Hardcover ISBN: 978-1-968250-00-3

Digital ISBN: 978-1-968250-01-0

GAME CHANGER PUBLISHING

www.GameChangerPublishing.com

**Dedicated to the memory of my incredible mother,
Laurel Seiler.**

*Your love, light, and relentless positivity shaped who I am.
I miss your energy every single day, and everything
I do carries a piece of you with it.*

ACKNOWLEDGMENTS

To my dad—Your steady presence, unwavering support, and quiet strength gave me the foundation to stand firm and the courage to bet on myself. You taught me the value of hard work, character, and keeping your word. Every step of this journey carries your influence — thank you for always believing in me, you will always be my rock.

To my brothers, Colton and Andrew—my roll dogs for life. You've been there through every win and every loss, always in my corner. Being your big sis is one of the greatest honors of my life. Thanks for keeping me grounded, hyped, and laughing through it all.

To Douglas Rupp—You believed in me, even when my dreams seemed far-fetched. Your guidance didn't just shape my career; it transformed my mindset. Thank you for always showing up, for never letting me settle, and for pushing me to rise.

To Kaleb Thornhill—Thank you for giving me the chance when it mattered most. You saw the potential in a different kind of financial coaching and trusted me to bring it to life. That leap of faith sparked purpose, passion, and an incredible friendship that I'll forever value.

Special thanks to **Bret Colson** for bringing my voice to the page with purpose, clarity, and heart. Your skill in helping me convey my story made all the difference.

None of this happens alone. I may be the one holding the pen, but this book was written with the strength, belief, and love of every person on this page.

READ THIS FIRST

Just to say thanks for buying and reading my book. I would like to give you a FREE copy of the *Train Your Money Companion Guide.* All the Tools from *Train Your Money* in One Easy-to-Use Framework!

Scan the QR Code Here:

SCAN ME

Train Your Money

AN EXPERT'S **WINNING PLAYBOOK** FOR YOUR **FINANCIAL SUCCESS**

Hillary Seiler

FOREWORD

BY JULIUS THOMAS, M.S.

Money is a focal point in most people's lives. However, financial health is much more than numbers in a bank account—it's an essential pillar of overall human well-being. Earning and managing money the right way reduces anxiety about our present and future, enables us to engage in joyful and meaningful experiences, and builds a financial legacy that protects the people we love.

As someone who has spent years dedicated to mental and physical health as a professional athlete, as a father committed to stewardship of my financial blessings, and who has experienced the pressures of financial responsibility, I understand how deeply financial matters affect all of us. The stress of managing and understanding finances can be overwhelming, but the right guidance can turn uncertainty into confidence, struggle into stability, and fear into empowerment.

That's why I wholeheartedly trust Hillary Seiler when it comes to financial education. She is one of the most gifted individuals I've encountered in this space, and *Train Your Money* is an essential confirmation of the powerful messages she has taught for many years.

Hillary doesn't just teach financial literacy. She transforms lives. Over the past eight years, I've had the privilege of watching her educate, inspire, and empower countless individuals. She has a remarkable ability to simplify complex financial concepts and turn them into practical, actionable strategies that fit each person's unique lifestyle.

What also sets Hillary apart is her elite understanding of finance and her ability to connect with people on a deeply personal and caring level. She has a gift for making financial education accessible and engaging, alleviating the stress often accompanying money matters. I've seen her captivate audiences by providing clarity to those who have never been taught the basics and others who need unbiased guidance on more complicated financial matters that can help them chart a responsible relationship with money for the rest of their lives.

Train Your Money serves two vital purposes.

First, it offers a roadmap for anyone seeking to improve their financial intelligence, whether you're just starting or looking to gain more advanced insights to manage your financial future. This book will help you assess your current financial situation and equip you with the foundational tools and strategies to achieve financial security and prosperity.

Second, when it comes to personal finance, there is always more to learn. Even those with a confident understanding of basic financial knowledge will find valuable insights in these pages. Much like Hillary's live presentations, which I've seen up close for many years, this book will leave you walking away with something new and impactful no matter where you are on the financial knowledge spectrum.

Train Your Money will help you move forward with clarity, confidence, and purpose. Hillary's expertise, passion, and dedication shine through in every lesson she shares. Her integrity, conscientiousness, and genuine care for others are why I am proud to call her a dear friend.

I strongly encourage you to take this opportunity to learn from one of the best.

Your future self will thank you.

Julius Thomas, M.S., played seven seasons as a tight end in the National Football League and is a two-time NFL Pro Bowler. Since retiring in 2017, he has become a cognitive scientist, executive coach, speaker, founder of Mastery Development, and co-founder of NESTRE Health and Performance, focusing on mental and cognitive strength training.

TABLE OF CONTENTS

INTRODUCTION
WHY YOU NEED TO TRAIN YOUR MONEY

People love talking about money—and for good reason. Money is the foundation of our society; we need it, want more of it, and go to great lengths to earn it. Unfortunately, for many, that's where the relationship ends.

Too often, we don't invest the time and effort to protect our money or make it work for us. I've seen countless people waste valuable time and resources by neglecting simple, smart financial habits early on. Without these habits, the difference between building wealth and not being able to build it can be significant.

That's why you must learn how to "train your money" to live the life you deserve. The earlier you learn these lessons, the better your life will be. What I will teach you in *Train Your Money* isn't about gimmicks or get-rich-quick schemes. It's about proven strategies that train your money to work for you by minimizing the downsides and maximizing the upsides.

You may already know some of what I will share; if that's the case, great! You're already ahead of the game. Regardless of what you already know, I'll fill in the gaps and give you the truth to make sure you're set for what's ahead.

* * *

My journey to financial literacy and, eventually, expertise started before I could even walk. While other kids were flipping through picture books and learning their ABCs, I was in my bouncer, pacifier in mouth, watching my grandpa across his huge office as he brokered deals and ran our family's tree nursery business in Gresham, Oregon.

Being the first of several grandkids, I spent a lot of time in that office during the day. But I also had the privilege of pulling up a chair at the dinner table every night and listening to my parents, Jeff and Laurel, talk about life. As our family grew, my mom made it non-negotiable that no matter how hectic our day was, we'd always sit down and eat together as a family. Those dinner conversations are some of my most vivid memories, because that's where I learned so many valuable lessons about money and life.

My parents were finance professionals, so they taught my brother Colton and me about money at a very young age. As we got older, as teenagers do, we put up a fight about coming down to dinner every night at 6 p.m. But my mom wouldn't budge. Looking back now, I'm so glad she didn't.

Our conversations about current events, politics, career options, economics, sports, dreams, what we planned to do with our lives, and, of course, money shaped me and my siblings in ways that took me years to appreciate fully. They were interspersed with my parents' beliefs about individual responsibility, ongoing learning, and always striving to be the best version of oneself.

Those lessons carried beyond our dinner table to all parts of our lives. I soaked up more important real-world knowledge at that dinner table with my family than I ever learned in high school. I learned how to navigate the business world, understand money and economics, set goals, and push myself to reach them. I learned how to dream big without fear and share those dreams with people who supported me in achieving them.

I was fascinated by all of it, and those dinner-table conversations are what led me to my career in finance. I poured myself into learning everything I could about how money works and understood early on that to make money the most effective tool possible, I would have to train myself and train my money to work hard for me.

Thanks to those conversations and a lot of hard work, I was confident I could do extremely well as a financial educator and money coach. So, at age 27, I started my first company. By 29, I had signed my first contract with an NFL team to teach rookies and young players financial literacy. As I made other people more successful, I became more successful, too.

Over the past decade, I've dedicated myself to becoming a trusted personal finance expert for more than a dozen NFL teams, several individual players, universities, NBA teams, and companies of all sizes across various industries.

Why am I telling you my origin story?

Two reasons.

First, I want you to understand that money is simple and complicated at the same time. You can grasp the basics with a little hard work, but if you want to do well in life, you must master the complicated part—your relationship with money.

Second, you have a unique money story different from mine, and I want to make sure it has a happy beginning, middle, and end.

* * *

Have I made mistakes with my money? Absolutely. I've made some big ones, and you'll hear about them later. Although they were setbacks, I chose to learn from them instead of beating myself up over them. Many of those mistakes became the foundation for the 10 pillars of financial literacy and money management that you'll find at the core of this book.

Train Your Money is more than just applying lessons that I've learned along the way. This is also a playbook about training you so you have an honest and healthy relationship with money for the rest of your life.

I was fortunate to have so many valuable dinner-table conversations about money and life in general. I want to share those conversations with you and perhaps inspire you to have important money conversations with the important people in your life, too.

At the very least, I want you to have the best foundational financial education to avoid setbacks and keep your money working in the best possible way for you. I'm going to give you tools that will help you talk about money with your family and teach the value of a dollar to your kids, family, and friends in the ways I learned about it.

My relationship with money started with my family at a dinner table in rural Oregon. Your journey is unique, but I promise that no matter where your journey takes you, *Train Your Money* is the best place to start that lifelong trek.

CHAPTER 1
CREATING YOUR MONEY MINDSET

Imagine you're a professional football player—a role model with fans who look up to you and cheer for you every Sunday. They analyze every play, track your stats more closely than brokers follow the stock market, and celebrate your success. You're living in a beautiful home, driving luxury cars, and enjoying a lifestyle many only dream of.

Not to mention, throughout your career, you have the chance to earn millions through salary and endorsements.

It sounds like the dream life, even if it lasts for a short window of time.

How short? It might surprise you to learn that the average career length of a National Football League player is just more than three years, and it is only slightly longer for NBA players, who average four-plus years, or the National Hockey League, whose careers average five years.

That also takes into account outliers in the NFL. For example, first-round draft picks average just more than nine years, and Pro Bowl players average about 12 years, assuming they stay healthy, which is always a challenge in any pro sport.

Not only is the NFL physically demanding, but it's also mentally demanding. Few things in life can prepare you for the fact that your season or career can end in a single play, changing your life in ways you can't fully prepare for.

Fans, the media, and anyone who has never played the game don't fully understand how challenging pro sports is. I must admit that even I was surprised when I started working with NFL teams a few years ago.

The mental and physical commitments required to perform at the highest levels in the NFL are daunting.

SWIMMING WITH THE DOLPHINS

When I started working with the Miami Dolphins, I walked into the team's practice facility ready to work—but nothing could've prepared me for the level of intensity I saw. I spent a few days each month there during the season, and it was clear from Day One just how demanding players' schedules are. Players and coaches grind relentlessly from July 15 through the end of the season. For some, that end comes in January, but for the talented and fortunate, it can stretch into early February with a shot at the Super Bowl.

There's no room for breaks, cheat days, or excuses. Effort is non-negotiable—you're expected to show up and perform at the highest level every single day.

Training camp days start with a 7 a.m. wake-up call and a team breakfast at 7:30 a.m. This is followed by a weightlifting session, a nutrition break, and practice leading up to lunch. Afternoons are consumed by watching film, another nutrition break, and various team meetings until dinner at 5 p.m. Evenings are filled with reviewing playbooks, stretching, another modest snack, and lights out anywhere from 9 to 11 p.m., depending on the player.

Saturdays are travel days for away games, but that doesn't mean players get a break if they play at home. They still have major team commitments to keep. Sundays are game days, and players must be at the stadium at least three hours before kickoff to prepare to perform when it's time to hit the field.

Per their collective bargaining agreement, players get one day off weekly, officially on Tuesday. Players sometimes get Monday off or have a light schedule of watching game film, recovery, etc. The flexibility depends on the head coach and the organization. The notable exceptions are bye weeks, when players get four days off, or when a player is injured and has a separate rehab protocol to follow.

Every organization is different, but that is a basic overview of life inside the bubble as an NFL player.

Now add the overlay of working in a job where just 2,000 other elite athletes are playing, knowing that thousands of others are waiting for the chance to claim your spot and live out their dream of playing in the NFL. Add to this that you are a high-profile public figure and that guys are cut at a moment's notice all the time. There are very few places to hide. It's a cost that comes at the price of fame at the professional level.

You can achieve financial security if you do the right things, but job security rarely exists unless you're all-time great quarterbacks Patrick Mahomes, Tom Brady, or a few other top stars in the league.

Staying in peak physical condition is one thing, but handling the mental pressure is quite another.

What I've learned from my time with the Dolphins and many other teams is this: Mindset is everything.

STEPS TO CREATING YOUR MONEY MINDSET

Although it's easy to see the athletic part in the NFL, you don't always see the mindset. However, winning on the field is all about mindset, and that same mindset drives my approach. You must have the same tools to succeed when you create an optimal money mindset.

Just like stepping on a field, to win at the money game, you must train hard, use what you've learned, constantly find ways to improve, and execute as well as possible to be financially successful. I'm an athlete, so I have insights into what it takes to succeed on the field. As a financial educator, I also have insights into what it takes to manage money successfully. The good news is that the mental skill sets are almost the same.

Both require creating positive habits that drive well-reasoned choices and consistently implementing what you know for long-term success. These are the foundational elements of discipline, which are essential as an NFL player and as your own financial manager. The bottom line is that you must train your money like a pro athlete trains for success.

To make this happen, you need to master four key components. To assist you, I've taken the lessons I've learned working with the pros and crafted a strategy to develop a winning money management mindset.

PART 1: DEVELOP AN OPTIMAL TRAINING PROGRAM

We are all exposed to money from a very young age. This happens before we understand what money is, how it works, and how to use it properly. At an early age, you might ask your parents for a new toy, to go to a theme park, or for them to buy you something even though you have no concept of money and what things cost.

Depending on our life lessons, we either grow and learn a lot about what things cost and how money works, or we remain rooted only in the rudimentary knowledge of mastering our money.

Every athlete has a training program to become a better player. They know what they need to do, when they need to do it, and how those choices shape their development. It makes a lot of sense to focus on the things directly tied to doing well in their career and life.

That's why I'm shocked when people don't invest time and effort in their relationship with money. Seriously, how can you accomplish your financial goals if you don't have an effective plan or program?

Just like an athlete needs a training program to perform at peak levels on the field, you also need an effective training program to perform at peak levels when it comes to your finances. And just like a physical training program where athletes train almost every day, you must create a money mindset regimen that you can execute daily, too.

Life tends to follow monthly cycles, so keeping a close eye on and refining your monthly budget should be the starting point. It's the foundation for creating a financial training program that brings structure and helps you execute your plan effectively. Breaking your finances down into manageable chunks, weekly or monthly, is the best way to stay on track and consistently manage your money successfully.

Your training program should be flexible so that it can grow and change as your income and expenses grow and change. No athlete sticks to the same workout regimen for any extended period. They constantly look for ways to improve and develop, and that's precisely what you should do.

You don't need a detailed plan right now—and chances are, you probably don't have one. Today, you can commit to developing your money mindset and training your money moving forward by using tools such as the *My Money Playbook* I've created and other readily available resources.

PART 2: EXECUTE CONSISTENT AND DISCIPLINED PRACTICE

When you've got a plan, it's useless unless you put it into practice every day.

I see it all the time—clients take that first step. They create a solid financial plan, map out a monthly budget, and set some critical goals. But as the excitement fades and discipline takes a back seat to desires, that plan gets pushed aside. They start making compromises and stop sticking to their plan within weeks—or sometimes even days.

Sooner or later, they hit a financial roadblock or get frustrated when they don't hit their long-term goals. That's when I ask them a question that might seem obvious:

If you are not practicing your money habits regularly, how can you expect to improve your financial picture or reach your goals?

Let's apply that question to an NFL player in training camp. Camp has started, the season is just around the corner, and he is working to make the team and earn a spot on the roster. He knows that nothing will be handed to him. That player will have to grind to get on the roster, prove his worth to the organization, and beat out other players willing to work just as hard to earn that roster spot.

Is there anyone among us who believes that missing a couple of practices, weight sessions, or going light studying the playbook will not affect his chances of making the team?

Of course it will!

Every repetition, practice, meal, and team session matters. If you aren't all-in during training camp, chances are you'll be all-out and looking for another place to play when the season starts.

Your money mindset must be exactly like that. Consistency and discipline are the keys. Every day and every dollar counts. If you fall down and deviate from the actions that serve you best, as many people do, don't beat yourself up too much. Instead, ask yourself why you fell short, learn where your weaknesses are, and get back to following your plan as soon as you can.

Small daily victories compound, but so do small daily failures. Consistency and discipline should be much easier if you're serious about being fiscally fit. You cannot succeed in football or your money mindset unless you have these habits in place, because every day counts.

PART 3: WORK WITH AN EXPERIENCED COACH

How many fewer Super Bowls do you think the New England Patriots would have won without Bill Belichick at the helm? Granted, Tom Brady is the GOAT, but he gave Belichick a huge part of the credit for the team's success over the better part of two decades.

An effective coach is more than just about the Xs and Os. They are masters of motivation, understand the value of constant improvement, and are responsible for creating a shared high standard that everyone must buy into. Winning is tied to many more things, but these are some basics coaches use to build a winning culture.

Money management mentors and head football coaches are not that different. We use many of the same strategies to help you get the results you want. Sure, you can commit to an excellent training program and execute consistently to win, but without an experienced coach in your corner, you're working a lot harder—and for way longer—than you need to.

Coaches are a primary source of education: a mentor, a leader, a skill builder, a motivator, and someone who will call bullshit when they see it. A great coach should be able to pull the best out of you while allowing you to find your personal path to greatness.

Partnering with the right coach can be the difference between building your own financial dynasty and settling for a life that falls short of what you deserve. Working with NFL teams as a Certified Financial Educator (CFEd) has given me the incredible opportunity to learn from some of the world's sharpest coaching and playing minds. The truth is, I've learned as much from them as the players I coach have learned from me.

During one of my coaching sessions a few years ago, I was holding rookie seminars on financial literacy and was surprised to meet a player with several years of experience in the league who attended. He didn't have to be there, and that piqued my curiosity, so I asked him, "Why do you come to my

Rookie Development seminars? You've been in the league for years."

His response was perfect.

"If I can take one additional nugget of information about finance out of your seminar," he said, "I've made myself better so that I can build future opportunities."

That thirst for knowledge was inspiring. Here was a man who had already enjoyed success in the league but wasn't done learning. He understood that the habits, consistency, and discipline that are hallmarks of success in the NFL are also essential when you're managing your money.

We continued to work together throughout the season and developed a great working relationship and friendship. We built trust in our relationship, and it all came together at the end of the season.

I held the last in a series of seminars in December. Although I was already impressed by this veteran player's humility and desire to keep growing, what he did that day told me, as a financial coach, that I had made a real difference. He joined me up front in the middle of the seminar, took the whiteboard marker from my hand, and started helping me teach the seminar. After a moment, I sat back and let him run with it.

That remains one of my favorite financial coaching memories. Watching the student become the coach and pass the same information to the next generation of incoming professional athletes was incredibly humbling.

But perhaps the greatest compliment he paid me was continuing to attend my seminars until the day he retired.

The lesson is this: Take advantage of the pros available to you. Tap into your financial educators, CPAs, financial advisers, estate attorneys, insurance agents, and real estate and lending professionals.

Just like in football, the best team wins the biggest games.

PART 4: FUEL YOUR EFFORTS

How an athlete fuels their body in sports is an integral part of how successful they'll be in their daily training and on the field. The same can be said for your financial life. Are you fueling your finances or taking away from them?

In the same way, they won't reach peak athletic efficiency by eating junk food every day, and you won't reach peak financial efficiency when all you do is spend, spend, spend.

That's why you must fuel your finances like an athlete fuels their body.

When an NFL player comes in after practice, chances are he just burned off 2,000 calories and needs to refuel his body. He is not only trying to refuel. He often tries to add muscle mass, meaning he needs to consume a lot more than he just worked off in practice. He must be strategic and pick foods to help him reach his goals. He is working with his nutritionist to ensure he is on the right track and eating the right foods to optimize his efforts.

Fueling his body is not always glorious. Sometimes, he eats two pounds of chicken, broccoli, and a protein shake instead of gorging himself on a couple of Big Macs, a ton of fries, and a chocolate shake. The Big Mac meal is a trap because it sounds mouth-watering, but it does nothing for him. In fact, it might starve his body of what it needs while altering his energy levels and metabolism.

Nutrition for NFL athletes is carefully planned for every meal and snack, with the biggest goal being to create strength and energy that can sustain players through rigorous practices and 60 minutes of game time every Sunday.

In the same way, fueling your finances includes educating yourself on money basics, making deposits into your savings and investment accounts, purchasing a home, opening a business, or setting yourself up for retirement. You are in this game for 40 or 50 seasons or more, so constantly fueling those efforts to create the healthiest financial scenarios is essential.

Just like athletes eat meals and snacks one sitting at a time, you fuel your finances by taking an active approach to developing and improving all aspects of your financial picture one step at a time. You need a sustainable, viable, and long-term plan to play the game to retirement.

Training your money and creating an optimal money mindset doesn't need to be a convoluted exercise. You can keep it simple as long as you follow the strategies I've outlined here. Develop an optimal training regimen, execute it consistently with discipline, work with a team of experienced financial pros, and feed your financial knowledge and actions one bite at a time.

Scan the QR code to unlock your Chapter 1 guide now.

Want all the tools in one place?

Download the *Train Your Money Companion Guide* to access resources for boosting your Money Influencer IQ.

FIRST STEPS TO CREATING YOUR MONEY MINDSET

You will not master financial literacy overnight. It takes a long time to understand how money works, and you must keep investing in knowledge, which is just as important—if not more so— than where you put your money.

If you don't have good money mindset skills right now, that's OK. Most people don't, and knowing where to start can be overwhelming and discouraging.

When you're beginning your money mindset journey, the best place to start is with several fundamental questions about your current relationship with money.

Answer these honestly, and you'll take the first steps to creating a baseline to build your money mindset.

1. How would you describe your current relationship with money in terms of how much you know about it?
2. How much time do you invest in growing your understanding of how money works?
3. Are you intimidated by money and worried you might get taken advantage of by others?
4. Have you ever been taken advantage of because you either trusted the wrong person or didn't fully understand the right way to approach your finances?
5. Who do you go to for money advice? Is it a professional adviser, a family member, or a friend?
6. Do you currently have a monthly budget?
7. What long-term goals do you have for your financial security?

8. How disciplined are you when it comes to money?
9. What is your biggest weakness when it comes to money? Do you spend recklessly? How often do you experience buyer's remorse?
10. What kind of shape would you be in financially if your income streams ended tomorrow?

CHAPTER 2
DEFINING YOUR MONEY INFLUENCERS

From the moment you're born, you have a relationship with money. Early on, it's controlled by the people around you, but as you grow, you gain the freedom to shape your own connection with it. That relationship can be smart and healthy—or it can be destructive and costly.

The key to building a strong relationship with money is understanding what drives your decisions, good and bad. When you know your motivations, you can take control now and secure your financial future.

THE COST OF MAC AND CHEESE

My mom used to tell a story to my friends about my special affinity for mac and cheese that started when I was still in diapers. I used to get a little embarrassed when she started telling it to my college friends and co-workers as a young adult, but then it dawned on me that this story was a perfect example of how our relationship with money is created and influenced before we even fully understand what money is.

The story goes like this: I had just turned one when my mom scooped me up for one of our favorite activities—grocery shopping. What she didn't know was that I'd spent the morning in the garage with my dad, who was always working on one project or another. That particular morning, though, he smashed his fingers and let out some very colorful language.

As my mom tells it, I picked up on things quickly at that age, including the ability to mimic and repeat words. I was a talker at an early age, typically one of the first proud-parent moments for many moms and dads. But in this case, not so much.

Apparently, I was also a headstrong child and was confident I was the boss of everything, even though I could barely walk. Combine these things with a trip to the grocery store, and magical memories happen.

I was in the shopping cart and saw one of my favorite foods at the time on a nearby shelf: good ol' mac and cheese. Since I was in charge, I reached out and put a box of it into our cart. Turns out that wasn't on Mom's shopping list that day, and she politely but firmly took the box out of our cart and put it back on the shelf as she told me, "No, not today, Hillary," like *she* was the one in charge.

I didn't take that rejection too well, so I grabbed another box and put it in the cart. Mom quickly took it out of the cart and put it back on the shelf, and we repeated this little power struggle a few more times before she pushed our cart down the aisle so I couldn't reach my beloved mac and cheese anymore. I wasn't going to put up with this grocery store coup, so I stood up and, at the top of my lungs, screamed a memorable word that my dad had taught me earlier that day.

"SHIT!"

I know you've been in grocery stores when youngsters acted out the same way. As a bystander, you're slightly amused and slightly taken aback, and although you try not to look, you focus on the mom or dad to see how they'll handle it.

My mom was mortified after my defiant outburst. My dad didn't know it then, but he was about to become an accessory after the fact. As for me, I just wanted my mac and cheese, even if it cost a million dollars. One dollar or a million, what did it matter? I didn't know about money then, including that you had to pay for stuff. I just knew what I wanted and was willing to do whatever it took to get that creamy, cheesy box of goodness.

My mom always ends the story by telling people that she contemplated leaving me in the store all by myself after that outburst. Not practical at the time, but it was somewhat understandable in that situation.

This is such a great story now because it is a metaphor for all of our interactions with money as adults. We see something we want. We often do whatever it takes to get it and think about how to pay for it near the end of our desires instead of at the beginning. For example, if I knew that box of mac and cheese cost a dollar at the time, but I didn't have a dollar to pay for it, my mom and I would have spared our fellow shoppers a lot of drama that day in the store.

It's a great story now, but it was a painful lesson for me and a reminder that we all must live within our means daily. As adults, many of us operate the same way.

We learn how money moves, but we're so often seduced by cheesy goodness that we set aside discipline in favor of short-term gratification. When we're not educated, or if we're not told "no" often enough, we develop bad habits at an early age. Those poor habits will land us in poor houses unless we figure out the right way to make money work.

THE ROLE OF MONEY INFLUENCERS IN YOUR LIFE

Everyone knows what social media influencers are, but how many of you know what money influencers are? Simply defined, they are the people, products, activities, and lifestyle choices that shape your money habits. As a small child, I knew how good mac and cheese tasted, so I was influenced to spend my mom's money to satisfy my desire for more of it.

Money influencers have been around for hundreds of years in one form or another. Before electronic media existed, newspapers ran ads, hucksters sold medicinal tonics door-to-door, and county fairs were full of salesmen demonstrating gadgets and potions from the four corners of the world. Radios brought influencers to the masses, with people we trusted hawking everything from toys, candy, automobiles, war bonds, and more. Sponsors who wanted to be associated with popular radio shows of the day attached their names to those shows and their celebrity hosts, hoping they would sell more goods and services.

Television changed the game again, and the stakes grew even higher. Companies sold everything from cigarettes and vacuum cleaners to sodas, clothing, kitchen gadgets, and countless other products to millions of people.

That worked well for money influencers for several decades until the dawn of the internet at the turn of the 21st century. It has been a full-on free-for-all since, with millions of sales channels now available to anyone with enough gumption, hard work, and confidence to put themselves in front of a global audience at a fraction of what it costs to use traditional legacy media. How we consume music, television shows, opinions, and news in all parts of our lives has changed forever, often with nothing more than our cell phones to get what we want.

The competition for eyeballs and attention is more intense than ever. Money influencers and social media influencers are often the same. The Kardashians, Taylor Swift, Justin Bieber, Joe Rogan, Logan Paul, and a legion of others have tens of millions of followers, and every one of them is trying to influence you to buy something based on their endorsements.

Then there are the viral moments that are completely organic and capture the public's eye for no discernible reason.

You are bombarded relentlessly in the hopes of gaining your precious attention. Because once they have your attention, they can influence you. And once they influence you, they can influence your money habits by trying to sell you something.

Young people are no different. The mac and cheese effect is still in play, but so are Baby Sharks, K-Pop bands, pre-teen gamers, and teen fashion influencers who have figured out how to win the game. They all understand the nature of contemporary connectivity and are brilliant at exploiting it as influencers.

The point is this: We're all exposed to money influencers at an early age, even before we understand how money works and how to use it properly. We fail to realize that the lessons we learned—or didn't learn—back then still play a big part in how we spend, save, and use money today.

Do you remember your first memory with money?

What is your mac and cheese story?

What about the first time you got an allowance and you could use your money to buy a snack at a 7-Eleven, save up for hot and trendy shoes or clothes, or buy a gaming subscription?

Do you remember the rush of borrowing your parent's car and putting some gas in it so you could go hang out with friends or just cruise and enjoy the freedom that a bit of money in your pocket affords you?

What about the rush you got after buying a T-shirt of your favorite band or a jersey or cap of your favorite sports team?

And finally, what about those times when you realized that the only way to get the nicer things in life meant you'd have to get a job and make money before you could spend it?

All of these things influence your early impressions of money.

You're overwhelmed with money influencers, but the most important ones are those in the house you grew up in. Your mom, dad, and siblings are your most important money teachers and influencers. That can be limiting at the outset in single-parent households, which comprise about 30% of families today.

If your family members set an example of responsible money use, you got a far greater and more honest education than all the other money influencers who have dropped in and out of your life. If that wasn't the case, there's a good chance you still struggle with money issues no matter how long ago you moved out to be on your own.

Sooner or later, you must learn that there are consequences when you swipe, insert, or hand over a little piece of plastic or enter your card information online. It's all too easy, and it's all designed that way on purpose.

Even though I didn't like it at the time, hearing "no" in that grocery store was one of the most powerful money lessons I ever learned.

THE ROOKIE AND THE LAMBO

Social media is a highlight reel. Nobody puts their bad stuff online. Yet we still suspend common sense and buy into the notion that everybody's living a grandiose, exceptional life. That perception versus the reality we see when we know all the facts is stunning. It paints a horrible picture of money influencers that can set you back quite a bit if you buy into the BS.

I had an NFL player who was a client a few years back. He was on the bubble as a rookie, which meant he had a good chance of not making the team. During the summer before his rookie year, before he signed his contract, I saw on his social media that he was driving a Lamborghini.

Initially, I pulled my hair out, because we had met just a month earlier and discussed what car he would buy. Suffice it to say that that car was not a Lambo. Given the financial uncertainty in his life, he couldn't afford it. So, when I saw his post, I reached out to him.

"Where did the car come from? Because I know we didn't talk about spending $200,000 on a car."

"Hi, Hill," he said. "Don't worry, it's just a rental, and I only wanted to take it out for a weekend."

Perception versus reality personified.

Although I was relieved, I still gave him a mini financial coaching moment by reminding him to get rental car insurance, because an accident would have wrecked a lot more than his pricey rental toy. In his position, he had earned the right for a test drive and was simply enjoying some of the perks of a potential NFL career. It was all good in that context.

However, to those not in the know, his social media was a flashy video of an NFL player about to sign his rookie contract and rolling up to his new house, also in the video. What viewers didn't know was that not only was the Lambo a rental, but the house was, too.

It's a good thing he held off, because even though he signed a contract, he was cut mid-season and didn't get picked up by another team. His NFL paychecks stopped immediately. If there's a silver lining to being cut, it's that he avoided making a bad purchase and saved himself a lot of money—and a lot of stress—since he likely would've had to sell it at a loss.

THE MONEY GAME IS STACKED AGAINST YOU

The desire to influence others has existed as long as civilization itself. The tribal need to belong has been drilled deep into our DNA from the time we lived in caves when there was strength in numbers.

You will not win the 24/7 game that money influencers play. The best you can do is to be as smart as possible to minimize negative influences on your financial well-being. You've got to rise above the FOMO—the fear of missing out—and understand that there are simply too many ways to spend your money. Accept that you will miss out, and be OK with that.

However, don't think of it as missing out. Think of it as practicing delayed gratification now to enjoy incredible rewards later on. Reframing your money influencers over the long term will bring a much-needed perspective on a healthy way to manage your money.

For example, you work hard every day, and when dinner rolls around, you want a fast and easy meal while you rest and recharge. If you're tech-savvy and statistically in the 18-40 age range, it's easy to call GrubHub or Uber Eats. However, you're paying not only for the meal, but also the tip and the service and delivery fees on top of that, all of which can quickly add up. That $30 meal can easily reach $45 or more. If you do that twice or three times a week, you're committing financial malpractice!

What if you used these services one fewer time per week? Setting aside all the add-on fees, if you cooked your own meal at a minimal cost of about $15 instead of a $45 outlay, you'd save more than $110,000 by investing those small amounts and letting them compound over 30 years.

It adds up, especially if you can do without multiple money leaks such as HBO, Amazon Prime, or Netflix subscriptions and in other areas of your life. There are cheaper ways to get goods and services if you must have them, such as family accounts, introductory discounts, coupons, or other lower-priced options.

You don't have to take my word for it. The internet is full of calculators to help you plug in your money and budget situation to illustrate these kinds of savings.

But all these numbers do no good until you develop the correct habits, discipline, and mindset and learn to recognize your triggers and money influences.

Resist the temptation of knowing you can click a button and have thousands of dollars' worth of whatever you want to show up at your door in less than 24 hours. I know how tempting—and, honestly, how sexy—that sounds, but that's exactly how the system is stacked against you. It's terrible for your financial mindset.

There is more installment debt than ever before because we're being buried by more choices than ever by sophisticated marketers who understand the nature of how we think. They are more than happy to exploit our weaknesses to line their pockets.

As I write this book, I am an old millennial in my late 30s. I didn't get a cell phone until I was 14, and even then, it was a Nokia where texting was a hassle. I didn't have easy internet access, Siri, AI, or Google. I was shielded during my formative years, which gave me the chance to develop strong money habits without the constant pressure of today's money influencers.

They're coming for you, and they aren't going to let up. What you allow yourself to consume from mass media, social media, your social circle, and society's constant push to sell you something means you must be insanely aware of how you're being manipulated.

Awareness is the key, and discipline is the strategy if you hope to win financial battles for the rest of your life.

EXERCISE: RAISING YOUR MONEY INFLUENCER IQ

1. What things currently tempt you to spend more than you planned? Are there any specific marketing tactics or social pressures that stand out?

   _____

   _____

   _____

2. Do you feel like your family background or cultural norms have played a role in how you view and manage your money?

   _____

   _____

   _____

3. Do you ever feel like ads get you? Ever bought something on a whim after seeing an ad?

   _____

   _____

   _____

4. Do friends' spending habits ever make you feel the need to keep up?

_____

_____

_____

5. Sales and discounts: Can you resist a good deal, even if you weren't planning to buy?

_____

_____

_____

6. FOMO (fear of missing out)—Does it lead to unplanned spending for experiences?

_____

_____

_____

Scan the QR code to unlock your *Money Influencer's Guide* **now.**

Want all the tools in one place?

Download the *Train Your Money Companion Guide* **to access resources for boosting your Money Influencer IQ.**

CHAPTER 3

SETTING FINANCIAL GOALS

What are your dreams? What do you want to do with your life? Where do you want to go? How much money do you want in your bank account?

These are all financial goals. The funny thing about goals is that we're always setting them in our heads. We all have things we want to accomplish. The tricky part is turning those goals into actionable steps.

THE SMART GOAL METHOD

One of the fastest ways to reach your goals is with the tried-and-true SMART Goal method. It's a standard across industries, and it can make all the difference in how—and when—you hit your financial targets.

SMART is an acronym that stands for the following:

S **Specific:** Clearly define what you want to achieve. Be as specific as possible.

M **Measurable:** Establish criteria for tracking progress and determining when the goal is achieved.

A **Achievable:** Given your resources and constraints, ensure the goal is realistic and attainable.

R **Relevant:** Align the goal with broader objectives or long-term aspirations to ensure its significance.

T **Time-bound:** Set a deadline or timeframe for completing the goal to maintain focus and urgency.

SMART Goals help you create clear, actionable, and trackable objectives. Once you create your goal, it's time to do the work.

In 2019, I worked with an NFL player interested in owning a barbershop. He decided he would cut a check to his brother to open and operate it, and he would be a silent partner. I loved this idea for him and asked him to get clear on his goal and bring me a summary of what that goal would be. This is what he brought me.

"I am going to open a barbershop in [XXX] location with my brother. We are going to have 5-7 chairs and split the revenue 50/50."

This was a great start and something for us to build on. After seeing this, I wanted to dive deeper into his goal and flesh out more details, including adding benchmarks. You must set benchmarks in goal-setting to assess progress, so we decided to sit down and build his SMART Goal together.

Here is how we altered his goal to be far more cohesive, achievable, and trackable, all while hitting the five SMART Goal criteria.

"I will open a barbershop with my brother as a co-owner within 12 months. We will take the following steps to open our shop: My brother will manage the business on-site as the head barber and staff manager. I will be the business manager and provide the necessary start-up costs up to $200,000 to start the business. The barbershop will be in [X] location, and we will lease the space. Within the first year, we will hire 3-4 barbers, filling up the full capacity of the space by year two for a total of 8 barber chairs.

My brother and I believe in community, and we want to provide a space for people to come and enjoy a little downtime while getting a fresh cut."

Here is how this outline aligns with SMART Goals:

Specific: Open a barbershop with my brother as co-owner, where he manages on-site as the head barber and staff manager, and I handle the business management and provide up to $200,000 in startup costs.

Measurable: Lease a space in X location, hire three to four barbers within the first year, and fill the space with eight barber chairs by year two.

Achievable: Ensures the start-up costs and hiring plans are realistic and within our budget and capabilities.

Relevant: The goal aligns with our belief in community, aiming to create a space where people can relax and get a fresh cut.

Time-bound: Complete the setup and open the barbershop within 12 months, reaching the full capacity of eight barber chairs by the end of the second year.

This goal set him up to start tracking what he needed to do to make this idea a reality.

Goals do not always have to be huge, or what we refer to as "big rock" goals; those can take years or require large capital investments.

Goals can be simple with shorter time frames as well. For example: I want to save $500 in six months to take a weekend trip to the beach, or I want to pay off $3,500 of my student loan debt in the next 12 months. You are winning in the goal-setting game as long as you have a measurable and specific goal that you will focus on and hold yourself accountable to in the time frames you set.

Just like anything life throws at us, most goals do not follow a linear path, and life can get in the way.

I set a goal for myself in my early 20s, which was to buy my first house by the time I was 25. That was a huge financial goal and one I wanted to hit. I almost did it. I was one month past my 26th birthday when I closed on my first house—and the kicker, it almost didn't happen.

At 25, I had saved enough to put a down payment on a $275,000 house—a goal I was beyond excited about. I was taking this on solo, so staying financially secure was my top priority. For three years, I worked 60 hours a week, saved nearly everything I earned, and managed to put away $50,000 to make this dream a reality.

My SMART Goal:

Save $20,000/year for three years so I can put 20% down on a new single-family home in Beaverton, Oregon.

My goal was concise, measurable, and something I was passionate about. I focused on it and gave it everything I had, but outside influences taught me a tough lesson that made reaching my goal harder.

Six months before closing on my new house, my partner, whom I had been with for four years, was turning 30. As a surprise, I took him to Las Vegas to celebrate. It was a three-day trip that I planned, budgeted, and prepped for. The trip was set, and the cost was supposed to be around $1,500.

After three days in Vegas and $8,000 later, I had to rethink a few things. Here's what happened and how my SMART Goal was thrown off track.

Our $1,500 budget for a three-day trip was a huge budget, one for which I had saved for over eight months as I was also working towards buying a home. On the first night of our trip, he asked if he could use some of the birthday money to have dinner with his brother, so I set aside $500 in spending money out of the budget for him to use. I gave him my credit card, and off he went.

Unbeknownst to me, during that trip, he used my credit card multiple times without my consent.

I remember getting on the flight home and checking my credit card transactions. I panicked because I thought someone had stolen my credit card information. I was stunned when I saw $1,500 at a club, $1,300 at Tom Ford, $800 at the Hard Rock, $200 at a steakhouse, and a lot more. When I figured out he had spent over $8,000 of my money, I saw my dream of owning a new home go up in flames.

Although I wasn't a financial coach yet and was learning as I went, I thought I had a pretty good handle on money—which, for the most part, I did. What I was not prepared for was the reality of money, goals, and relationships. I never imagined that someone I trusted would take advantage of me and take my money without talking to me first.

I had to pivot quickly while simultaneously juggling my financial goals and my relationship. I had to figure out how I was going to recover $8,000 and get that back into my bank account to close on my house the following spring. This was 2012, and my significant other was not working because the job market was still recovering, and he was in between jobs. It fell on me to pay off the credit card and recoup the money for my house.

Our trip took place at the end of October 2012, and my house was set to close in May 2013. That meant I needed my down payment ready to present to my lender by April 1. I had six months to save up the money I needed to recoup and be ready to put $50,000 down plus closing costs on my house. I was forced to reframe my financial goals in hopes of making my home-buying dreams a reality.

I worked a sales/commission job that allowed me to hustle harder and longer hours and make a little more money. That is exactly what I did. I made it my goal to limit my spending to the necessities and save an extra $1,750 per month for the six months—giving me a total of $10,500 by April.

It was a long road, mistakes were made, and in the end, I was able to bounce back and buy my first house. Those first six months in my new home? Let's just say it was a lot of mac and cheese and ramen dinners.

Our goals are often shaped by the people and things we surround ourselves with, and that can sometimes throw us off course. To overcome those hurdles, it's important to use the tools you have and pivot when needed. Some goals won't happen on the timeline you planned—or might not happen at all—and that's OK. As life evolves and priorities shift, be open to adjusting your goals and embracing the changes along the way.

To access the Goal Setting Tools, download the *Train Your Money Companion Guide*.

Scan the QR code:

CHAPTER 4
DEVELOPING A BUDGETING SYSTEM

Budgeting is easy to define.

It is the process of knowing how much money is coming in and going out of your life and then applying common sense to ensure your income does not exceed your outgoings on a regular basis.

For some people, the idea of creating a budget is downright terrifying. That's why so many avoid it, even though running from it only worsens their financial situation. They'll even go so far as to label it something less intimidating—cash flow, money management, burn rate, fund control—you name it.

Call it whatever you want, but here's the bottom line: If you don't figure out how to manage your money effectively on a daily, weekly, and monthly basis, you're setting yourself up for big trouble.

Like all other things connected to financial fundamentals associated with training your money, budgeting is all about discipline and consistent habits that build in guardrails to ensure you are responsible with your money, whether you make $25,000 or $500,000 a year.

Your cash flow management system is the cornerstone of a healthy relationship with your money. Although most systems share common principles, the real key is building a unique, flexible system tailored to your financial priorities and obligations. When you create a system that truly works for you, sticking to your budget becomes much easier because it's your plan—not one that someone else forced on you.

Everyone manages money differently. There are endless tools, courses, books, apps, and resources to help, but at the end of the day, the success of your budget comes down to how well you design a system that serves as the foundation for everything else you do with your money.

In simple terms, suppose you want to buy a new car within the next 12 months and know you want to put down $10,000. That requires making budget choices that affect how you spend the rest of your money. You'll need to devise a plan that reduces spending in one area of your life to set aside $800 to $1,000 a month to reach that goal. Or you'll need to increase your income by that amount to reach that budgeting goal, perhaps by picking up a side hustle or liquidating other assets.

MY BROTHER'S SYSTEM

My brother Andrew wasn't great with money early on. It came in and went out just as quickly, with no real accountability. But a few years ago, he decided to turn things around. He wanted to get out of debt and create a better life for his daughter. Once he found a reason that mattered enough, discipline and better money habits started to fall into place.

What's interesting is that even with endless resources out there, my brother built a system that worked for him—completely unique to his style. No budgeting apps, no Excel spreadsheets, no paper. He created his own system using notes on his phone, and that's how he got out of debt.

Andrew is paid weekly, and from this, he broke his financial obligations into weekly incremental payments to mirror his income. He works in four-week blocks, and in his notes, he writes out *Weeks 1 through 4"* and adds a section for incoming bills and when they are due. Each bill is placed under the week it's due, and when that week pops up, he makes it a priority to ensure those bills get paid. After everything is paid, he has a section for leftover cash that he transfers into his savings account, which he can use for major purchases and unexpected financial hits that everyone experiences.

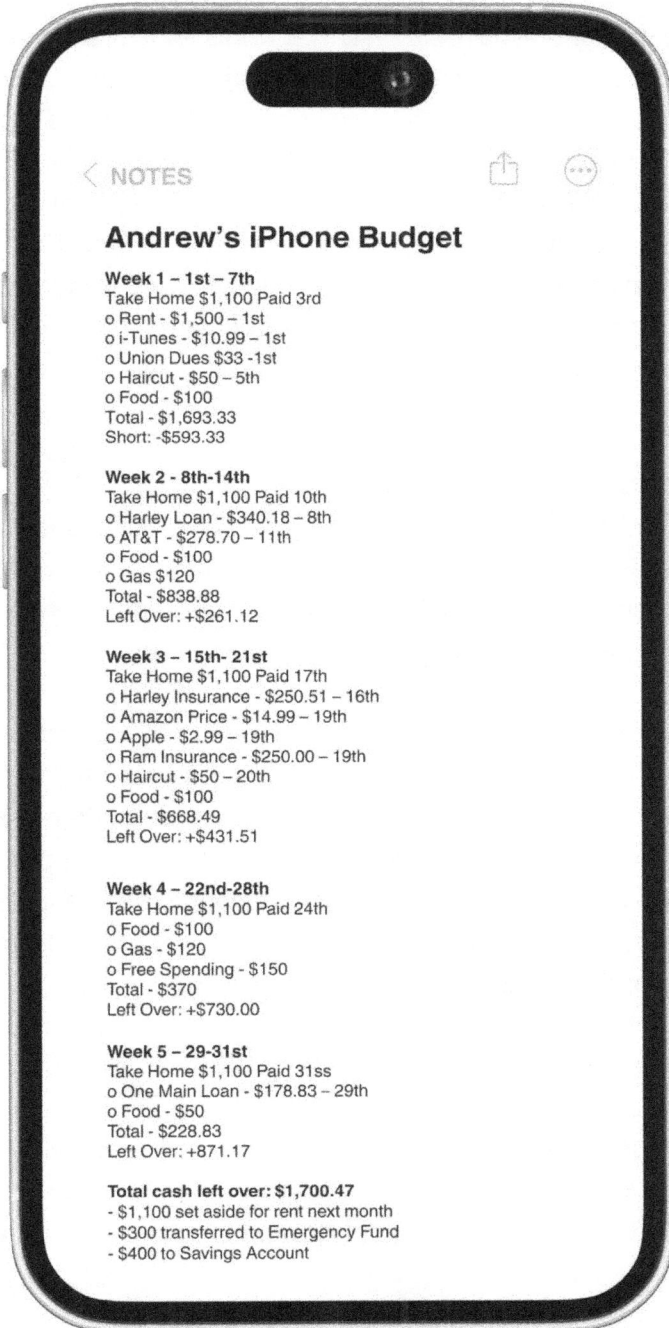

Andrew's iPhone Budget

Week 1 – 1st – 7th
Take Home $1,100 Paid 3rd
o Rent - $1,500 – 1st
o i-Tunes - $10.99 – 1st
o Union Dues $33 -1st
o Haircut - $50 – 5th
o Food - $100
Total - $1,693.33
Short: -$593.33

Week 2 - 8th-14th
Take Home $1,100 Paid 10th
o Harley Loan - $340.18 – 8th
o AT&T - $278.70 – 11th
o Food - $100
o Gas $120
Total - $838.88
Left Over: +$261.12

Week 3 – 15th- 21st
Take Home $1,100 Paid 17th
o Harley Insurance - $250.51 – 16th
o Amazon Price - $14.99 – 19th
o Apple - $2.99 – 19th
o Ram Insurance - $250.00 – 19th
o Haircut - $50 – 20th
o Food - $100
Total - $668.49
Left Over: +$431.51

Week 4 – 22nd-28th
Take Home $1,100 Paid 24th
o Food - $100
o Gas - $120
o Free Spending - $150
Total - $370
Left Over: +$730.00

Week 5 – 29-31st
Take Home $1,100 Paid 31ss
o One Main Loan - $178.83 – 29th
o Food - $50
Total - $228.83
Left Over: +871.17

Total cash left over: $1,700.47
- $1,100 set aside for rent next month
- $300 transferred to Emergency Fund
- $400 to Savings Account

It's not fancy, but it does the job quite nicely for him in about 20 minutes weekly. The point is that he has a system. It works for him, and he's become a lot more financially responsible using a system he *wants* to use. He has gone from reckless and unaccountable spending to a person who manages his spending habits and saves as much money as possible.

One of the most significant benefits is something that can't be fully measured but is huge in the way he now budgets his money. That something is peace of mind. Armed with a simple but effective strategy, he doesn't obsess over or get rattled by money issues anywhere near as much as before. Because he has a plan that works, he can handle the unexpected more rationally and calmly.

THE BUCKET SYSTEM

One of the NFL players I coach uses a variation of this system. It works for him because he's bought into a process that makes sense to him, and he helped design it. Unlike my brother, he's not the kind of person who likes to track every penny. Instead, we came up with a bucket system that fits his style.

He knows he's a spender, and for him, seeing one big pot of money is like a giant green light to spend. Once we recognized this, we took a different approach. Now, he has several accounts—or "buckets"—where he allocates his money each time he gets paid. He likes knowing how much is in each bucket, and this setup has reduced his temptation to overspend because the smaller buckets feel more manageable—and less enticing to dip into.

He has one bucket dedicated to bills and monthly expenses. Others are for emergency expenses, car payments and maintenance, personal savings, and one for free spending, which covers entertainment, vacations, dining out, and similar lifestyle expenses.

Each time he gets paid, he moves money into each bucket based on a percentage of his income. As his money management skills improved, we automated the process instead of doing this manually each month. His employer made that easier by allowing him to set up direct deposits into multiple accounts each month.

Part of this process also includes checking that the right allocations have been made to the appropriate accounts and that the balances align with what he believes they should be. Now, he has a highly effective budgeting process that takes him less than 10 minutes every two weeks.

I can't stress enough how important it is to check your account balances at regular intervals as part of your budgeting process. Without this, you lose critical oversight and accountability.

THE EXCEL MASTER SYSTEM

My dad was a stickler for saving money. He raised me to think strategically about money and to play the money game to win from as early as I can remember.

I started working a few hours a week at a family restaurant when I turned 14, which jumped to 20 hours a week when I turned 15. I didn't need to work that much, but I wanted to work that much because I liked the money. I wasn't too worried about managing my money at first, but when taxes started to kick in, I paid more attention.

My dad has always been a numbers guy, but I can't say the same for me as a kid. In my teen head, numbers sucked, and I wasn't particularly fond of them except for the amount on my paycheck. However, as I was a minor, when my parents opened my first bank account at U.S. Bank, they had to be on my account with the requirement that my work checks had to be "managed" a certain way. That was my first introduction to a budget.

I had to put at least 50 percent of my net income (the money I took home after taxes) into a savings account, which was non-negotiable. I couldn't push back if I wanted to because my dad had to drive me to work daily. So, without his help, I wouldn't have a job.

My dad gave me the freedom to decide where the other 50 percent of my income would go.

From the start, I had to choose how to spend my money, and if I ran out of money before the end of the month, it was on me. My parents made it clear they wouldn't give me any additional money because I had a job, and "that was that" in their minds.

I quickly learned how fast money can disappear. Between Slurpees, movies, gas for my friends' cars, fast food, and other "essentials," it was a constant balancing act from the start.

After a few months of that "broke" feeling, two weeks into one particular month, I had one of my family's famous dinner table conversations that helped me reframe my ideas on money management at the time, which still influences how I budget my money today.

Because my dad viewed money strategically, looking for ways to win, he first taught me to track my spending. Ugh! Accountability. A bit of a pain, but it was critical for my success.

I was only 15 and didn't want to track my expenses manually, so my dad introduced me to Excel and helped me set up a spreadsheet system. My first budgeting system tracked my income and expenses and looked like this:

Income	Date	Amount
Pay Check	5/1/2002	$ 127.41
Pay Check	5/15/2002	$ 136.85
Total Income		**$ 264.26**

Expenses		Amount
50% to Savings	*5/1/2002*	*$ 63.71*
Movie Ticket	5/3/2022	$ 7.99
Popcorn/Candy	5/3/2022	$ 8.99
Lunch/Drinks @ School	5/4/2002	$ 3.99
Gas	5/7/2002	$ 12.99
Lunch/Drinks @ School	5/8/2002	$ 3.99
7-Eleven	5/10/2002	$ 6.50
50% to Savings	*5/15/2002*	*$ 68.43*
Gas	5/16/2002	$ 10.00
Lunch/Drinks @ School	5/17/2002	$ 3.99
Doc Martins	5/20/2002	$ 59.99
Lunch/Drinks @ School	5/27/2002	$ 3.99
Total Expenses		**$ 254.55**

This forced me to pay more attention to where my money was going, and soon, I started playing to win (thanks, Dad!) when I saw just how much I was spending monthly. By age 16, I had given myself monthly spending limits with a goal attached. I wanted to save 75 percent of my after-tax money. In my mind, winning was measured by a growing savings account balance.

Although the numbers are different now, I still use the same basic system in my business and personal life. It's a detailed strategy that works for me because I'm wired that way. Depending on how you think and what your goals are, your budgeting approach may be different.

The key is to have some kind of approach. Understand that you can be flexible as you go until you refine a budgeting system you are comfortable with, depending on how you view money.

If you've never created a monthly budget before, I challenge you to try it—just once. Build out a full budget down to the last penny and stick with it for a month. It's the quickest way to really understand your spending habits. You'll discover what kind of system works for you, how you spend your money, and what your good and bad habits look like.

But don't approach this as some dreaded exercise designed to cut out fun and block your spending. Instead, consider budgeting your ally—a tool to help you chase those big dreams while balancing your day-to-day life.

Be realistic, honest, and reasonable with yourself. If you build a budget based on unrealistic expectations, you only set yourself up for frustration and wasted time. Budgeting can be a tough reality check, but it's also a necessary one. Like going to the doctor, you need to identify the symptoms before fixing the problem. Creating a budget is how you address financial issues now so they don't become bigger problems later.

DEVELOPING YOUR BUDGETING SYSTEM

Getting started is the hardest part of any new habit, but implementing various action items will start you down a path to optimal financial health. Remember that the system you use, whether it's the three kinds I've used as examples in this chapter or another system that works best for you, requires consistency and dedication to detail. You must also develop a strategy that is easy to understand and implement based on your temperament and lifestyle.

I suggest you use the following questions as starting points on your budgeting journey. Do the work, pay attention to your thoughts, and be honest.

- **Track your spending and income** for one to two months if you have an irregular cash flow, and budget for irregular expenses by identifying periodic costs such as car maintenance or holiday gifts. Estimate the yearly total, divide by 12, and save that amount monthly in a dedicated account. This helps you handle these costs smoothly without straining your budget.
- What is your **big overall motivation** for budgeting?
- **Decide on your priorities.** How do you want to spend and save your money in a way that is meaningful to you? What can you cut and reallocate using existing money in your budget?
- Define important big-dollar **short- and long-term goals** (family vacation, saving for a house, a new car, target dollar amounts for your 401(k) and savings accounts, etc.). Consider setting up buckets so you can allocate funds to each month to track your progress.
- **Create a sample budget.** Ask yourself if you are happy with this and if you can stick to it. If you chafe at the numbers you've come up with, chances are you'll fail. I've included a simple two-page template below to give you a sense of how easy this can be.

Budgeting is about give and take, priorities, and creating a contract with yourself that you can not only simply live with but that you can also embrace wholeheartedly. Get after it and play the long game. You are in this to win with your money.

One of the most effective and simple tools I encourage clients to use is the following budget planner from my company's My Money Playbook Planner. The playbook is a six-month money management guide with financial tools and exercises that also teach readers the right way to deal with money.

To access the My Money Playbook Planner, download the *Train Your Money Companion Guide*.

Scan the QR code:

CHAPTER 5
MANAGING YOUR FINANCES WHEN A CRISIS HAPPENS

When somebody close to you dies, you go numb. You will cry. Depending on the circumstances, you may feel life is not fair. But a part of you does go numb. You don't quite know how to feel, whether it's unexpected or you watch a person you love dearly slowly slip away.

Your priorities are completely reshuffled. You may shut down or completely pour yourself into your work. Everyone reacts differently. Things like money, prestige, and material possessions mean less. The way you think changes as you contemplate your own mortality and how fragile life truly is. And the deeper you care about the person you lose, the more intense those feelings are.

We all go through it sooner or later, including me.

THE CALL THAT CHANGED MY LIFE

College was a turning point in my financial life. Before college, I had a great financial foundation with good habits in place. I knew quite a bit about how to manage my money, and combined with discipline, I developed a great relationship with my dad about everything regarding money. I felt really good about where I was at with my finances.

Armed with this confidence, I never suspected that something could derail my efforts when it came to my finances and my life. I couldn't have been more wrong.

At 19 years old, my world imploded. I was on summer break from college, working a full-time job, when I got the call that changed my life. It was my dad who told me that my mom, Laurel, was in the hospital. Then he said two things I'll never forget.

"The doctors don't know what's wrong, and we don't know if she's going to make it."

I was beyond stunned. I don't remember what we talked about next. I had to cope with the fact that my mom went from walking around one day, not feeling great, to going into the ICU at Emmanuel Hospital in Portland, Oregon, with a gut-wrenching prognosis that nobody saw coming.

Many of you reading this have probably gone through something similar, so you have an idea of the intense emotions everyone in my family felt over the following days and weeks. My mom spent 17 days in the ICU while doctors tried to figure out what was wrong with her. They didn't have any answers, which made a bad situation even worse. Without knowing what was wrong, they couldn't effectively treat my mom, and it tore up our entire family to know that. However, after a month in the hospital, the doctors stabilized her, and she was able to come home.

We were grateful that she felt better, and secretly, we hoped the worst was behind her. None of us even remotely suspected that this was the start of a long battle that my mom would eventually lose.

That was the first time in my life that I genuinely started to panic about money. Until then, my parents had done everything they could to make my life as easy as possible. I didn't have everything I wanted, but I did have everything I needed. Although I wanted to be financially independent at 19, in the back of my head, I knew if I ever got into deep trouble, I could go to my parents for help.

However, after spending 30 days in the hospital, my parents were inundated with medical bills. They had great medical insurance, so things could have been much worse. But even so, there were still a lot of co-pays and out-of-pocket expenses to deal with, and it wasn't long before my parents' bank account balances started to dwindle dramatically.

That summer, I went from having a college fund to pay for school and working summer jobs to supplement living expenses to taking out student loans and working a full-time job to help relieve some of my family's financial burdens. It felt like I was living in the *Twilight Zone*, but in the moment, you just keep moving forward the best way you can.

COPING WITH THE EMOTIONAL TOLL

My mom was in a coma for those first 17 days at Emmanuel Hospital. That was the first time a doctor told me my mom was going to die. Her lungs had stopped working, and several other serious issues were further weakening her. They put her on a respirator and told us that if her lungs did not drain and she was unable to breathe on her own in the next few days, she may never be able to breathe on her own again.

It was the first time in my life that I felt like I had no control and zero ability to help the person I was closest to in the world. My mom was my best friend, so that helpless feeling was crushing and triggered all sorts of intense feelings ranging from sadness to anger. And it wasn't just me. We had one of those houses where my mom always welcomed our friends and neighbors, so when she got sick, I saw how much she had also touched their lives.

As bad as it was for my brother and me, it was even worse for my dad. My mom was the rock of our family. She kept it all together, running our household and a couple of businesses. She was sassy and a fighter but still the kindest soul you'd ever meet. She complimented my dad perfectly. He was the provider, the badass, and a big old softie when it came to my mom.

They met in college. My dad saw my mom in business class and told a friend, "I am going to marry that woman." It was that kind of a relationship. They were each other's perfect match, and he knew it from the first time he laid eyes on her.

And so it was, with very little notice, that when my mom went into the hospital, his whole world turned upside-down. He was losing the love of his life, and I did the best I could to be a person he could lean on. It's the most heartbreaking thing in the world, watching your parents sitting in the hospital together, holding each other's hands and talking, knowing that they might be separated at any moment.

* * *

Eventually, the doctors were able to diagnose my mom with an auto-immune disorder. Her body was turning on itself, slowly destroying from within the person I cared about more than any other. The cruel part was that even though they had a general idea of what was wrong, they couldn't diagnose it with a high degree of accuracy. That was agonizing.

She was an anomaly, and while the amazing teams at Oregon Health & Science University (OHSU)—a leader in auto-immune research—did everything they could, because she was an outlier, they also sent her to specialists nationwide.

My family and I spent more time in hospitals with my mom between 2006 and 2013 than we did out of them, including one stretch that lasted seven months. Near the end, she was fragile, weighed about 90 lbs, had trouble walking and talking, and was in a lot of pain when trying to eat because the muscles in her throat that allowed her to swallow were constantly under attack by her immune system. Her condition was unpredictable. We never knew when it would flare up or with how much intensity.

My dad lost his best friend, the love of his life, and the person he wanted to grow old with on April 24, 2013. The world loves a happy ending, but sadly, that was not to be the case in our case.

I appreciated how hard all of the doctors and medical staff worked to cure my mom, but in the end, because her condition was so rare, that translated into massive hospital bills, extended hospital stays, trial drugs that did more damage than help, and emotional stress that took a toll on all of us.

We're a close family, and that financial toll taught us all lessons that we would have preferred not to learn, so I'm sharing my story with you.

MY MOM'S LEGACY

My mom wrote all of us letters the Christmas before she passed. To this day, that letter is the single most important thing in the world to me. Parts of the letter are private, and I'll never reveal what she wrote. But she also wrote something about money, and because it helped me and I know her words will help you, I wanted to share it with you now.

"Success and wealth are important but only because they give you a sense of accomplishment and allow you to do things that are worthwhile in life. Family is the most important thing in life. Don't let the pursuit of money, success, or your dreams supersede everything else. Without your family and friends, nothing is truly worth it. … Money is a tool, something to help you achieve your life goals. It should not be the life goal."

COPING WITH THE FINANCIAL TOLL

My mom's illness was emotionally draining in ways I could never have imagined. Aside from how it affected our family, we had hundreds of thousands of dollars in medical bills in just the first few years she was sick.

My dad's preparation, savings, and overall financial IQ allowed him to rebound financially after my mom passed. But it has still been an uphill financial battle. My dad had to completely reset his life at age 55 instead of enjoying the payoff of a well-financed and thoughtfully planned retirement he and my mom were working toward. They had done everything right, but there was no way they could have planned for a long-term crisis like this.

As for me, I continued on in college and financed my education by taking out student loans for the three years after my mom got sick. I chose to work because I didn't want to leave college with more debt than I needed to, and I paid for my living expenses through my job, which didn't always cover the bills. I did not want to ask my dad for a single cent, so there were weeks when PB&J sandwiches were my every meal.

Watching our family tragedy unfold, I decided I needed to up my game and learn everything I could about money. I needed to gain a lot of financial intelligence, and one of the first steps I took was to start an emergency fund. Until that point, my dad had taught me some things, but for the most part, I was dealing with money as I went. I changed from a reactive mindset to a proactive mindset to get out in front of as many potential pitfalls as I could before they struck.

I'm also experienced enough to know that no matter how much you plan and save, there are some things you simply can't handle the way you'd like when they rudely appear. In those cases, the best you can do is soften the landing.

As I write this, my dad is now 67, and thanks to my brother, who is a Certified Financial Planner, they put together a plan that rebuilt his wealth over 11 years so that he can now retire if that's what he wants to do. We're more fortunate than many people who never recover after an experience like ours.

HOW TO BUILD AN EMERGENCY FUND

Even if you don't have extra money to set aside now, you always have time to invest in understanding how to put your money to work for you.

Building your financial intelligence is like going to a gym and hitting the weights to build muscle. Think of that muscle as knowledge, and the more of it you have, the better positioned you are to do the heavy lifting of putting your money to work for you when you are in a position to do so.

Building your financial IQ goes beyond basic budgeting or saving; it's about developing a deep understanding of how money works, including investing, credit, risk management, and long-term financial planning. Financial intelligence equips you to analyze your financial situation, identify opportunities, and make strategic decisions that align with your goals. In a world where financial landscapes constantly change, developing financial intelligence is critical for staying on top of things that can lead to costly mistakes.

To build financial intelligence, you need to focus on education and awareness. Fortunately, there's no shortage of information to educate you on the subject. With some work, you can identify trusted sources of information and confirm the initial knowledge you access by broadening your efforts to include several sources, including books, online courses, and working with a financial coach.

Awareness is just as important. You must make conscious decisions to evaluate your financial habits and modify them as you learn more or as macro conditions change. This is not a static part of your life; you should treat it as an ongoing habit requiring dedicated work.

With a stronger financial IQ, you can approach money decisions with confidence, working proactively instead of getting caught short by acting after the fact.

Awareness and education are all about understanding the bigger picture, whether it's maximizing your investments by considering risk tolerance or strategically using credit to your advantage.

Financial intelligence enables you to look beyond the immediate impact of a financial choice and see its long-term implications. For example, rather than viewing credit cards as a short-term solution, you recognize how they can build credit history when used wisely or burden you with debt if mismanaged.

Ultimately, financial intelligence helps you take control of your financial future. The more you understand how financial systems work, the more you can tailor them to suit your life goals, such as achieving financial independence, buying a home, or building wealth to securely protect you and your family.

With a base of knowledge and habits that keep growing that base, you are better positioned to build your emergency fund.

An emergency fund is your financial safety net, protecting you from unexpected expenses such as medical bills, car repairs, or job loss. Without one, you risk going into debt or derailing your financial goals. In the case of my mom, it was all medical bills.

Having an emergency fund provides peace of mind. It is your first line of defense to prevent high-interest debt and helps you maintain financial stability during uncertain times.

6 STEPS TO BUILD YOUR EMERGENCY FUND

1. **Set a Savings Goal.** If you're just starting out, set an initial goal of 3-6 months of essential living expenses, including housing, food, utilities, and transportation. If you prefer, start with a smaller and specific monetary goal, such as $1,000, and build from there.

2. **Automate Savings.** The best way to create the habit of contributing to your emergency fund is to set up automatic transfers to a dedicated savings account from each paycheck. Even small, consistent contributions add up over time.

3. **Choose the Right Account.** Keep your emergency fund in a high-yield savings or money market account for accessibility and growth. Avoid riskier investments so the funds are there when you need them the most.

4. **Redirect Extra Income.** To accelerate your emergency fund-building efforts, use tax refunds, bonuses, and windfalls to boost your emergency savings.

5. **Cut Back Temporarily.** Temporarily reduce discretionary spending to jump-start your savings. Buy into the fact that short-term sacrifice offers long-term financial security.

6. **Stay Disciplined.** Don't deviate from your fund-building efforts to go on spending sprees. Don't drain your fund for non-essential and impulse spending binges. Also, clearly define what constitutes an emergency, such as medical bills, job loss, or urgent repairs.

CALCULATING YOUR EMERGENCY FUND NEEDS

Your emergency fund is the financial safety net that you tap into when unexpected expenses or larger financial crises like a job loss or a large medical bill affect you. Your emergency fund is unique to you, and you'll need to think about how you live and where your money goes as part of this exercise.

Before we start, let's answer some frequently asked questions so you understand how to create an appropriate emergency fund for your circumstances.

How much do i need to save each month?

Until you reach your target goal, including the number of months you want coverage for, the right answer is as much as your current financial conditions allow. If your first goal is a two-month emergency fund and the total amount is $5,000, you may be able to set aside $1,000 a month, meaning it will take you five months to reach that first plateau. At $1,250 a month, it will only take you four months. Obviously, the more you can dedicate, the quicker you'll build the financial security you need to protect yourself. The important thing is to start stacking your balance as soon as possible.

How many months should i have saved in my emergency fund?

Your financial situation will be a BIG factor in how many months of expenses you need in your emergency fund. The answer is different for everyone, but financial planners strongly suggest that you target 6-12 months of savings. However, your scenario may dictate a different number of months.

If you're single and young and lost your job today, could you easily find another one? If so, having 3-6 months of expenses in your emergency fund should be a good starting point.

If you're married, the sole income earner for your house, and losing your job or being unable to work would truly alter your financial picture—then 9-12 months of expenses in your emergency fund should be the goal. If you have people depending on you, having roughly a year's worth of wages saved can be a game-changer.

If you work a sales or commission job where your income fluctuates monthly and based on the time of year, 6-12 months of expenses in your emergency fund should be the goal.

Should I Have a Separate Bank Account for My Emergency Fund Money?

Yes! We like using a high-yield or money market savings account for our emergency fund. Keeping your emergency fund balance separate from your savings accounts and regular checking accounts will help you keep track of your balance and progress. Plus, high-yield and money market accounts pay more interest than a traditional savings account.

Can I Have Too Much Money in My Emergency Fund?

Yes again! Holding 24+ months of expenses for emergencies removes your ability to invest and build wealth. There is such a thing as too much when it comes to your emergency fund. Your goal is to find balance in the 3-12 month guidelines based on your financial situation.

BUILDING THE FRAMEWORK FOR YOUR EMERGENCY FUND

To create the right target amount for your emergency fund, you'll need to separate your expenses into three categories.

- **Necessary Expenses** are all of the things you MUST pay for every month. These include rent or a house payment, utilities, insurance, food, etc. They are non-negotiable and must be accounted for without fail.
- **Non-essential Expenses** are your discretionary costs. Things like dining out, Starbucks, streaming subscriptions, and other lifestyle expenditures that you can eliminate in a crisis fall into this category.
- **Additional Expenses** are those that come due on a bi-monthly, quarterly, semi-annual, or annual basis. An Amazon Prime or Costco membership, renter's insurance, or other bills that pop up once or twice a year fall into this category. You'll still need to budget for them, but you generally have discretion on whether to do that monthly or plan to pay them in a lump sum when they come due.

You'll come up with a total monthly expense when you add these three categories. Depending on your financial situation, you'll clearly understand how much you'll need to save to build your emergency fund to an appropriate level. Simply multiply your monthly amount by the months you want to target. Experts agree that a minimum of 3-6 months is a good initial target, but saving for more months than that further insulates you from potentially negative money catastrophes.

To access the *Emergency Fund Calculator* and supporting video resources

Scan the QR code:

CHAPTER 6
HOW CREDIT SCORES WORK

By this point in your life, you've heard the term "credit score," and you may have a rudimentary understanding of what it is and how it affects your finances. But like many people I meet and counsel, you probably have knowledge gaps and misconceptions about some parts of credit scores and the way they function.

Few things can complicate and add costs to your life, like a bad credit score, so it's critical to understand what you must do to protect and maintain a high score by every possible means.

Let's start with the basics by answering some simple questions.

WHAT IS A CREDIT SCORE?

A credit score is a number generated from your credit reports that indicates how likely you are to pay back various types of loan debt you take on. Companies use credit scores to make decisions on whether or not to extend credit to you in the form of mortgages, car loans, credit cards, and other similar credit products. Scores are also often used by landlords as part of a tenant screening process and, in some cases, by employers as part of the hiring process or when providers issue various types of insurance.

Your credit score is determined by using a scoring model to create a number typically between 300 and 850. A higher score makes getting new loans at more favorable interest rates easier.

It is often referred to as your FICO score, named after the Fair Isaac Corporation, which created a credit scoring model that is widely used in finance. The scoring model uses data from companies reporting your credit usage to agencies. The agencies use this information to generate a credit report on you.

What Are the Factors Bureaus Use to Determine Your Credit Report and Credit Score?

Various elements are weighted slightly differently depending on the agency, but all generally take into account the following factors:

- Bill-paying history
- Current unpaid debt
- The number and type of loans you have open
- How long your loan accounts have been open
- How much of your available credit you're using
- New applications for credit
- Have you been late on loan payments or had a debt sent to collection, foreclosure, or bankruptcy? How long ago?

Who Oversees Credit Scores?

There are several companies that aggregate your credit information. Businesses report your credit usage to these agencies, and they use their own scoring models to calculate your credit score. That's why you don't just have one credit score—each model weighs and calculates things differently.

Although plenty of credit reporting agencies are out there, three dominate the financial world: Equifax, Experian, and TransUnion. Most companies report credit information to all three (and sometimes others), but they're not required to. Similarly, when companies "pull your credit" to assess your credit risk, they might check with one, two, or all three agencies to build your credit profile.

What is Considered a Good Credit Score?

Credit scores generally range from 300 to 850 and are broken into tiers. A FICO score of 850 is pretty much unreachable, but many people shoot for an 800 score, including me, as you'll read about below. That's an admirable goal, but in most cases, a credit score of 740-760 and above will get you the most favorable terms when taking out a loan.

Tiers vary slightly by reporting agencies. For example, Experian uses the following ranges to generally classify the amount of risk associated with someone applying for a loan.

- **800 to 850:** An excellent credit score indicative of a very low-risk borrower
- **740 to 799:** A very good credit score that will still produce highly favorable terms for a borrower
- **670 to 739:** A good credit score, but you may get hit with less favorable terms because you are at an elevated risk.
- **580 to 669:** A fair credit score that will definitely have an impact on how much it will cost to borrow money
- **300 to 579:** A poor score will make borrowing money much more costly. In some cases, lenders will not even consider a loan when someone has a score in this range.

How Do I Raise My Credit Score and Avoid a Bad Score?

Both of these things are easy to achieve in theory but more challenging to achieve in real life unless you're disciplined and understand what you can and cannot do to change your score.

Raising your credit score doesn't have to be complicated—just stick to common sense. Pay your bills on time, avoid taking on too much credit debt, and keep your debt-to-credit ratios in check. Another key factor is how long you've had credit. Lenders want to see a solid history of responsible credit use over several years.

Big red flags for your credit score include late payments, charge-offs, bankruptcies, or other major negative events. Although these issues will matter less over time, it can take a while to recover. For example, a bankruptcy can stay on your record for up to 10 years. If you've had a significant credit event and plan to borrow again, check your state's laws so you're clear on how it might affect you before applying for a loan.

Another must-do is to check your credit reports regularly. By law, you're entitled to a free copy of your report from each of the three major agencies once a year. You can also pay for additional copies if you want to check more often. When you get your report, review it carefully and flag any errors. If you spot something off, you can file a dispute to correct it.

A great strategy is to rotate between the three major agencies, requesting one free report every four months. This helps you keep a close eye on your credit throughout the year. It's also a smart move because fraud and identity theft are serious threats today. By staying on top of your reports, you can catch any suspicious activity early and take action fast.

MY QUEST FOR AN 800 CREDIT SCORE AT 21

Every family has habits and rituals passed on from generation to generation. If your mom or dad was an athlete, chances are you played a lot of sports growing up. If your parents were into the arts in a big way, you probably went to several museums, concerts, and other cultural outings. This also applies to the types of family vacations you went on, the foods you ate, whether you attended church, etc.

My family is no different. In addition to some of the other things I mentioned, my dad required me to be financially literate at an early age. He schooled me in various ways while I was young, but things changed when I turned 18, and he had "the talk" with me.

At 18, my dad sent me to our local bank and instructed me to apply for a credit card. He told me at the time that everything requires credit, so it was best that I learn as much as I could as early in life as possible. I realize now, more than I realized then, that my dad was not kidding!

He told me he could lecture forever but that the only way to learn about credit was to step into the real world, start building my credit history, and aim for the best possible score I could before I left for college. Although my informal education started a few years before, my real financial education started the day I stepped into my local U.S. Bank branch.

Despite all my dad had downloaded to me at that point, I was somewhat intimidated and didn't know much about what I was doing. However, banks love it when you want to establish credit with them, so they were very helpful when I applied. Ten days later, my first student Visa card arrived in the mail with a $500 limit. That doesn't sound like much now, but back in 2005, I was 18 with another $500 in my pocket, so I felt like I was rolling in cash at the time. Of course, teens have little impulse control, meaning my first instinct was to spend some of my newfound money.

My teen brain thought it was a great and logical idea. My dad did not.

He put the brakes on my spending spree before it ever got started. He reminded me that I was about to be a broke college student and that if I didn't have a way to pay back the money I put on the card, I was going to be in trouble from the outset. That's because banks will do just about anything to make sure you pay them the money you owe them in a timely manner.

At our dinner table one night, he gave me the speech everyone new to credit needs to hear. There was a lot more to it, but basically, it went something like this.

"You should not ruin your financial life over $500. Credit is king in the world of finance. Everything requires credit, and making mistakes with it can blow up your entire financial picture."

No stress there. Thanks, Dad.

Then he added: "Credit is actually pretty easy once you know how the system works and how to play the game."

My dad is all about strategy. Play smarter, not harder. He then gave me his blueprint for using credit, which has been a winning strategy ever since. Shortly after, inspired by his talk, I decided I wanted an 800 or higher credit score.

My dad laid out a game plan to reach that goal using his blueprint, which consisted of three simple rules.

MY FATHER'S 3 RULES FOR AN 800 CREDIT SCORE

Rule 1

Never miss a credit card payment. Always pay in full and on time. Even missing a payment by as little as 30 days could mean a hit on your score. The more times you miss, the greater the damage it will do.

Rule 2

Never max out any credit card. It will drop your score. You can use up to 30 percent of your limit or less. If you go over that threshold, your score will drop.

Rule 3

Use your card every month. You have to be consistent if you want to build a credit score. You can't get a credit card or other revolving line to just let it sit in a drawer somewhere. Agencies and banks want to see regular usage to create a track record of responsible use.

About 30 days after I got my card and started using it, I got my first credit card statement. Again, I had no idea what I was looking at, so I went back to the dinner table with my dad.

We went through his guidelines for using credit to make sure I hit them all.

Rule 1. That was easy because I paid the credit card bill in full and on time. Thanks to my first dinner-table chat, I only put about $30 on it that month, so I made sure I could easily pay it in full.

Rule 2. I didn't fully understand my credit utilization ratio at the time, but I understood the math. A $500 limit x 30 percent meant my budget was $150. I didn't understand why I was given a limit of $500 but was only supposed to use 30 percent of it.

As my dad explained, it boiled down to financial impact and risk. Banks can only see what you spend, and if you overspend or max out your credit cards, you look like you don't know how to manage your finances. That may not be the case, but it is a red flag, fair or not. To them, the numbers are black and white, and there's nothing to read between the lines or understand. A banking algorithm, such as the FICO score, has parameters. All it understands is that 30 percent or more usage on a credit card looks like financial mismanagement, and your score drops. Ouch!

Rule 3: I had one month in the books, which was not a track record of consistency... yet. But I was armed with that information and was paying attention to what consistency with credit should look like. I used my card correctly and paid it in full that first month. Now, I needed to rinse and repeat the cycle every month for life.

Then, my dad took it a step further.

LONG-TERM BUDGETING IS CRITICAL

That night, we created a plan of how I would spend money for the next 6-12 months using my credit card. We agreed it would pay for my gas at $20-$30 a month and groceries at about $100 monthly.

I stuck to my dad's spending rules and blueprint for the following year. It wasn't as hard as I thought it would be because it became part of my routine. I kept a close eye on my transactions and ensured I didn't overspend—there was no way I could handle a $500 credit card bill while in college.

At the time, I worked 20 hours a week and used student loans to cover tuition and books. I didn't have any extra money to throw at overspending. If I had slipped up, I would've gone straight into debt. It was tough enough to manage my other bills without adding a huge credit card payment.

At the end of that first year, as a newly turned 19-year-old college freshman, I went from a 0 to a 720 credit score by paying a few bills on my monthly credit card. Truth be told, I didn't have to charge $100-$150 a month on the card. I could have only charged $10 monthly, and I still would have built a good credit history. But my dad and I created a good long-term plan, and I was determined to stick with it.

If you want a similar result, the key is to pick one recurring expense like Netflix, your cell phone bill, or groceries, and put it on your credit card. Pay it every month in full to demonstrate consistency to the reporting agencies.

Things changed for me halfway through my sophomore year. My bank automatically increased my credit limit from $500 to $1,000. That's a good thing, right?

I didn't know they could do that, so I had a small panic attack, and—you guessed it—I called my dad. He quickly calmed me down and explained that because I was being responsible with my credit card and demonstrating that I was using it consistently, they were extending me more credit because of my perfect track record. He told me to think of it as a reward for good behavior.

I was 19 and getting rewarded for good credit behavior. I was winning!

My dad went on to say, "A credit line increase is just that. Let them raise your limit, but you don't have to use it. It's additional money you can access in case of emergencies, which we hope you never have to use. However, it's there and good to have."

He also said, "Don't change anything you've been doing. Stick to our plan. Keep your spending under $150 a month because you don't need to add more credit card debt, and besides, you cannot afford to spend more on your card right now anyway. Stay consistent every month, and let's look at things in about a year."

Solid advice that seemed obvious, unless you were an inexperienced credit user like I was.

Another year passed, and I stuck to our plan, feeling better because I was now two years into my credit-building journey. When I reached this milestone, I checked my credit score, and it had jumped to 775!

Was I stoked? You bet I was. I was only 20, spending less than $150 a month on my card, and never paying the bank a penny of interest because I paid my bill in full every month.

When my score crept up to 780, U.S. Bank raised my credit limit again, this time to $2,500. That was more than all my monthly bills combined. Now that I knew more about how the game was played, I was ecstatic because it meant I had a proven winning strategy for building a great credit score.

SUCCESS!

Fast-forward to shortly after my 21st birthday, and I hit my big goal. I became a member of the 800 Club. I felt like a rock star! It took me a little over three years, but with a lot of patience, discipline, and guidance from my dad, I did it. We were both proud of what I had accomplished.

Then, I faced another challenge. How do I keep my FICO score at 800? I was graduating from college soon, and the pressure of moving into the world after graduation presented some new challenges.

So I did what any girl would do in this situation. I went back to our dinner table for another talk.

I was worried my score would drop if I changed our blueprint. I knew as I left college that my spending habits had to change. With my dad's help, we changed things and adjusted to life after college. I got a couple of additional cards with $10,000 limits and started using them to pay for all my monthly essentials such as utilities, groceries, gas, insurance, cell phone, and streaming services.

Now that I understood how credit worked and how to work my credit limits, I started using my new cards to accumulate credit card rewards. I got pretty good at that, too. At 22, I took my first fully paid vacation using credit card points.

The three essentials—consistency, correct usage, and paying on time—never changed. Thanks to the discipline my dad instilled in me, I didn't go off the rails when I obtained credit lines of $25,000+ shortly after I graduated. I've never come close to using anything near that amount, but it's nice to know I could access that credit line in an emergency.

The education that my dad gave me took a little work. He set me up and changed the game for me from a credit perspective. I hope you have someone in your life who can give you expert guidance. But if you don't, you can do it on your own, much the same way I've shared with you.

Credit is a powerful tool, but it can be intimidating. If you don't manage it carefully, it's easy to lose control and end up in a financial mess that could take years to fix.

If you're just getting started, start small and keep it simple. That's exactly what I did. Focus on one purchase at a time, one month at a time. Stay patient, think long-term, and keep educating yourself about how to use credit to your advantage. There's no secret shortcut: Success with credit comes from having a plan and sticking to it. That's the real key to making it work for you.

Learn the rules and play the credit score game well. The money you save and the peace of mind you achieve are worth it.

Download the *Train Your Money Companion Guide* and get access to our credit mastery resources.

Scan the QR code:

CHAPTER 7
FAMILY MONEY DISCUSSIONS

Few topics have the potential to stir emotions as intensely as when families discuss assets. This shouldn't come as a surprise, but what is surprising is how far family members will go to avoid having conversations about this topic in the first place.

We were open about money discussions in my family, but the frequency and intensity of those talks grew when my mom got sick. Many families don't follow this line of thinking, keeping things private, which isn't unusual. That often stems from older family members' values and beliefs about how money should be handled and passed down.

There's no one-size-fits-all way to approach money conversations. After years of working with clients, I've learned that these are some of the most important discussions you can have with your spouse, parents, siblings, and other family members. Avoiding them can lead to distrust, frustration, and unnecessary tension. Open, honest conversations can make all the difference.

Whether or not your family talks about money, life is constantly changing, and those changes will inevitably influence your family dynamics and, with them, your money dynamics.

I've shared the circumstances of my mom's long-term illness and her passing when I was 26. Beyond the emotional devastation, it was financially crushing, especially for my dad. But because we were a close-knit family, we were able to have open and honest conversations over the years about how to face those challenges together.

Those discussions weren't easy. But since we approached money as a shared responsibility—something we all had a stake in—it made it possible to include everyone in those conversations. We faced the financial crisis as a team, and the result was not just getting through it but also creating a foundation for ongoing, honest money talks that we still have almost 20 years later. Despite the hardship of my mom's illness, it brought us closer and taught us the importance of working together on one of the most critical aspects of a healthy, thriving family.

Understanding what money we had, where it was going, and how it affected our family wealth helped us contribute and assist each other. This was building our family's net worth profile while allowing us to make decisions and close things out in case one of our family members passed.

The organization my dad and brother put into place for our family finances continues to make the tough conversations easier. Because of that open dialogue, we push ourselves to improve our financial choices. It is a win-win.

Every family's financial situation is unique, but there are practical strategies you can use to make financial conversations easier and more transparent. The depth of those discussions will depend on what your family feels comfortable sharing. At the very least, it's important to have open conversations about core financial matters, especially when preparing for the loss of a loved one.

Avoiding these conversations can leave your family unprepared. In my mom's case, we learned early on how critical it was to put some basic financial protections in place. Here's what we prioritized.

- **Assign beneficiaries to your bank accounts.** These beneficiaries can have access to funds that are payable on death, commonly known as POD. If the account holder passes, you can access or close out the account when you present a death certificate and an ID.
- **Update your will or trust at least every 1 to 2 years.** This is especially important if there have been major life changes, such as birth, death, divorce, or another major life event. If you have a financial team helping you build these documents, confirm how often they should be updated.
- **Start talking to your family members now.** If you're stuck on how to do that, here are several suggestions to open up critical discussions as soon as possible.

CONVERSATION STARTERS

Talking about money often starts with a few family members agreeing that it's time to have open discussions about the family's finances. But starting those conversations can feel uncomfortable, leading many to delay much-needed talks.

This hesitation can grow even stronger if it's clear that some family members tend to be emotional or resistant regarding financial goals and planning strategies.

Usually, one person takes the lead and sets the discussions in motion. Depending on the family dynamic, that could be a parent, a sibling, a third-party executor, or even a family attorney who helps open the lines of communication.

Figuring out what to talk about can also feel like a roadblock, especially in families where strong personalities, disagreements, or tensions about money are part of the history. It's a common challenge, but one that can be navigated with the right approach.

A GOOD STARTING PLACE

If you're in a family where discussions have stalled, consider using the following questions to guide an open and productive conversation about finances. The goal is to create clarity, understanding, and a shared plan for the future in a non-threatening way.

- What are the most important values we want to guide our family's financial decisions?
- How can we ensure younger family members are financially literate and prepared for the future?
- What plans should we have in place for emergencies or unexpected life events?
- Are there any unresolved financial concerns or questions we need to address together?
- How often should we check in as a family to discuss financial updates?

WHEN TO START

The best time to start talking about money with your family is *now*. It doesn't matter if you're navigating a big life event—like a marriage, a new job, or the birth of a child—or simply recognizing that financial transparency is overdue. The earlier you start, the better. These conversations are less about the ages of family members or life-changing milestones and more about building a habit of open communication.

HOW TO START
- **Choose the Right Time.** Schedule a specific time when everyone can be fully present without distractions. A relaxed setting—like a family dinner, weekend afternoon, or a casual Zoom call—works best. Avoid busy or high-stress periods, like tax season or holiday gatherings.
- **Set the Tone.** Approach the conversation with a collaborative mindset. Let everyone know this is about working together and creating a shared understanding, not assigning blame or control.
- For example:
  - "I think it's important for us to all be on the same page about family finances. Let's talk about where we stand and what the future looks like."
  - "I want to make sure we all feel prepared and supported, especially when it comes to big decisions down the line."
- **Make a Plan.** Outline what you want to discuss beforehand, and encourage everyone to bring their questions or concerns to the discussion. In addition to pressing family financial issues, in an initial discussion, topics might include:
  - Family savings or financial goals.
  - Estate planning—wills, trusts, or beneficiary details.
  - How to handle emergencies, such as medical bills or unexpected expenses.
  - Teaching younger family members about budgeting, credit, or investing.

- **Be Transparent.** If you're leading the conversation, be prepared to share. For example, if you're discussing estate planning, explain your decisions, such as why you chose a certain executor or how you intend to divide assets. If you're introducing kids to budgeting, share real examples from your financial life to make it relatable.
- **Focus on Solutions.** If challenges or disagreements come up, keep the focus on solutions. This isn't about dwelling on past mistakes but creating a clear path forward. I suggest bringing in a financial adviser or mediator for guidance if needed.
- You can also build momentum by gaining consensus on low-sensitivity issues and being prepared to compromise. Also, understand that some issues may need to be set aside in the short term until you can gather more information or have separate conversations to work on areas of disagreement.
- **Create an Ongoing Dialogue.** Money conversations are not a "one-and-done" effort. Because life constantly changes, your family's money dynamics will also change. To ensure that disagreements don't arise, minimize problems by making money conversations an ongoing conversation. Regular check-ins as needed help everyone stay aligned and adapt to changes.

HOW TO HANDLE CHALLENGING AND SENSITIVE SITUATIONS

Every family's money dynamics are different, but certain challenging and sensitive situations come up for a lot of us. Understanding these scenarios and having a game plan ahead of time can help you avoid unnecessary conflict. For example:

What if Your Parents Are Guarded About What They Want to Reveal?

It's common for parents to be protective when discussing finances. They may feel it's too personal or not want to burden you. Start by explaining why you want to have the conversation. Consider something like, "I want to make sure I understand things so I can help if needed or plan better for the future."

If they're still hesitant, ease into it with questions that feel less invasive, like asking about their experiences with saving or what financial lessons they wish they'd learned earlier. The goal is to create a space for open, judgment-free dialogue over time.

What if Family Members Are Not on Good Terms?

Tough family dynamics can complicate money conversations, but navigating them with care is still possible. Focus on keeping things fact-based and neutral. Avoid rehashing past grievances, and clarify that you're trying to plan or solve a shared issue.

For example, if there's tension about who handles what, suggest creating a financial road map or bringing in a neutral third party, such as a financial adviser, to help mediate and organize the plan. It's about finding a path forward, not dwelling on past issues.

How Do You Deal With Family Members Who Have Been Irresponsible With Money to This Point in Their Lives?

This one's tricky because financial habits are personal, and change takes time. Start by setting boundaries—what you're willing to help with and what you are not. You can also help them create a budget or share resources like books, apps, or coaching that could guide them. But remember, it's not your job to fix their financial mistakes.

Be supportive without enabling. If you're being pressured to cover for them financially, it's OK to say no. That's not selfish; it's protecting *your* financial health.

At What Age Should You Include Children in Discussions?

Start earlier than you might think you should. Kids as young as eight can understand basic money concepts like saving and budgeting.

By 14, involving them in conversations about household expenses, like groceries or saving for a family trip, is great. At 16, they should learn about more significant financial topics such as credit cards, loans, and how to manage their first paycheck. By 18, as they approach adulthood, they should clearly understand things like taxes, budgeting for independence, and the basics of long-term planning.

Adjust the depth of the conversation based on their maturity, but don't wait too long. Financial literacy is a skill, and practice starts at home as early as possible.

How Much Should Spouses Know?

Everything. Money is one of the top stressors in relationships, and keeping secrets about finances can break trust. Both partners should fully see income, expenses, debts, and financial goals. This doesn't mean you can't have separate accounts, but it does mean all decisions and details are transparent. A shared financial plan isn't about control; it's about teamwork. When both spouses are on the same page, navigating challenges and building a strong financial future together is easier.

What if You Have Disagreements on What to Do With Family Wealth?

Disagreements are normal, especially regarding big decisions such as investing, gifting, or legacy planning. The key is to focus on shared values and priorities. Ask yourselves, "What do we want this wealth to achieve? Is it about security, education, philanthropy, or generational support?"

If you're stuck, consider bringing in a financial adviser to offer an impartial perspective and help find solutions that honor all sides. The goal is to approach wealth as a shared resource, not an individual possession, and to build a strategy that reflects your collective goals.

What Are the Primary Roles and Responsibilities of an Executor?

The executor is critical in carrying out someone's final wishes as outlined in their will or trust. They're responsible for managing the estate, which includes gathering assets, paying off debts, filing taxes, and distributing inheritance to beneficiaries. It's a position of trust and requires a lot of organization and communication.

If you're asked to be an executor, ensure you fully understand what's involved because it can be time-consuming and emotionally taxing. If you're naming an executor, choose someone reliable, detail-oriented, and capable of handling potential conflicts among family members.

What Legal Rights and Responsibilities Are Good to Know in a Trust or Will Situation?

Trusts and wills come with legal obligations that everyone involved should understand. For example:

- **Beneficiaries** have the right to receive what's specified, but they also might need to wait until debts and taxes are settled.
- **Trustees** must act in the best interest of the beneficiaries, manage the assets prudently, and keep clear records.
- **Executors** must follow the will exactly as written unless it's legally contested.

Educate yourself on your role and responsibilities if you're part of a trust or will. Consulting an attorney to understand the details and avoid potential conflicts is always smart.

What Goals Should Children Have for Discussions With Their Parents?

Children should focus on understanding the big picture:

- **Wishes.** What do your parents want for their financial future and their estate?
- **Plans.** Are there wills, trusts, or directives in place? If so, what should we know about them? Are there specific wishes you have for family wealth or assets?
- **Preparation.** What information do we need to step in and help if needed (e.g., account details, insurance policies, or important contacts)? How can we help you manage your finances as you age?

These conversations are not about taking over but about being informed so you can support them when the time comes. The goal is to understand clearly, reduce surprises, and avoid family misunderstandings later.

What Goals Should Parents Have for Discussions With Their Children?

Parents should:

- **Educate.** Share financial lessons, values, and strategies to set children up for success.
- **Inform.** Ensure that children know where key documents and accounts are and understand your wishes regarding health care or estate planning.
- **Empower.** Create clarity and confidence for them to handle financial decisions when needed.

Make your children informed, not overwhelmed. An open dialogue helps ensure they're prepared to carry out your wishes and navigate responsibilities confidently.

Here are some specific questions parents should ask their children.

- What do you know about our family finances?
- What financial lessons or habits have you found most helpful so far?
- Are there areas of money management where you'd like more guidance?
- What are your financial goals for the next 5-10 years?
- How can we help you prepare for significant life events such as college, buying a home, or retirement?

What Essential Questions Should Siblings and Extended Family Members Ask?

Siblings can sometimes clash when it comes to money, and extended family members may be deeply intertwined in your immediate family finances. This may be because of a family business relationship or because they are recognized as having a high aptitude for family financial planning. If that's the case, consider these questions to open up a line of communication and avoid conflicts.

- What are your thoughts on handling shared family wealth or assets?
- How can we work together to ensure transparency and avoid conflicts?
- If someone needs financial help, what should our approach be as a family?
- How do we want to handle financial responsibilities for aging parents or shared properties?
- What steps can we take to ensure everyone is on the same page about financial decisions?

CHAPTER 8
PROTECTING YOURSELF FROM FRAUD

You've heard the adage, "It's not what you make. It's what you keep that counts."

Initially, this applied to ways to cut your tax debt, maximize your returns, and so forth. But in recent years, this has also been used more and more to avoid becoming a fraud victim.

As technology has advanced by leaps and bounds, especially in the field of artificial intelligence, a new breed of scammers has become more sophisticated than ever. International crime rings commit large-scale identity theft, hack into financial and government institutions, and steal private and critical financial information, using it to wipe out fortunes in the blink of an eye.

These hackers also sell sensitive information to other criminals, covering their tracks through sophisticated means, costing individuals and institutions billions of dollars in losses. And unfortunately, that trend continues to grow.

You've worked hard to build your wealth, and if you've figured out how to invest and have a long-term game plan to grow your wealth, part of that plan must also include making your financial information the hardest possible target for crooks to breach.

Part of this requires ongoing vigilance and education. I could list dozens of ways you can be scammed, and I'll mention some of the most common ones below. But as soon as law enforcement identifies how fraudsters steal from you, several new scams pop up to take their place. It's an ongoing financial cat-and-mouse game; you must play it well to avoid becoming a victim.

$55,000 GONE IN FIVE SECONDS

Seniors are the most predominant victims of fraud. They tend to be less sophisticated and more trusting, easily lured into revealing financial information that can leave them destitute with little hope of recovering funds.

But seniors aren't the only ones susceptible to fraud. It can happen to anyone, regardless of age, the amount of money in their bank account, or how prudent and responsible they think they are. It's a global problem, but in the U.S. alone, 13 million people were victims of identity theft in 2022, and there were $5 billion in losses due to fraud in 2023. The Consumer Financial Protection Bureau estimates that losses due to fraud are growing by about 20 percent annually, with no signs of slowing down.

You may think fraud only happens to other people who are careless. That's what one of my oldest friends thought, and it cost him dearly.

He is a busy executive who has worked for a large tech company for several years. My friend is a smart and savvy guy, but he's also slammed at work most of the time, putting out fires and dealing with complex, fast-moving issues more often than not.

One day, he got a call from a woman who identified herself as someone from the local Wells Fargo branch where he banked. It appeared to check out because the on-screen area code was local, so he didn't think twice when he answered the phone and took her call.

After a brief exchange, she said, "We want to let you know your account has been compromised. There have been some fraudulent transactions. Did you purchase XYZ?" It was the first part of a well-rehearsed and tested script.

Like all scam victims, she said all the right things to him, and he responded with some panic, assuring her he wanted to resolve this immediately. She spent 20 minutes on the phone with him, explaining the fraudulent transactions in detail, and telling him she would resolve the issue on his behalf.

She was good and reeled him in, hook, line, and sinker. At the end of their call, she explained that the first thing he should do was reset his account password to protect it and that she would email him instructions immediately to do just that.

As a busy executive, my friend is a problem solver, which he does all day at a lightning-fast pace. This was one more problem to solve, but it was accompanied by an added overlay of emotional stress and duress because this situation was personal.

He was anxious to resolve the breach as quickly as possible and with minimal damage to his finances, so he did exactly as instructed. Although he admitted to me later that something felt a little off, he pushed forward in the heat of the moment anyway. The woman continued their email dialog for several more days, slowly getting my friend to reveal more personal information. By the end of that week, she got answers to his security questions, user names, passwords, and more.

Once she had everything she needed, she reset his passwords and raided his accounts. It took her five seconds, and she stole $55,000 from him, draining his checking and savings accounts and maxing out the cash advance lines of credit on his bank credit cards.

Then she disappeared.

There's an even darker postscript to this story. It was considered consensual sharing of privileged information because he consented to give her access to his bank accounts. By doing this, he was not covered under banking fraud laws, whether the resulting transaction was fraudulent or not. Also, although fraudulent purchases qualify for protection, cash advances do not. He had no recourse to recover what he had lost, much like me giving my boyfriend a credit card and telling him to have a good time in Las Vegas.

Although I don't agree with all banking laws, banks can't be expected to pay for every mistake consumers make. Banks are careful in their disclosures when you open accounts, informing you that they will never call or ask for personal information. They also remind you about monthly statements, which we all glaze over after seeing them once or twice.

My friend and I have both learned that if you make a mistake with your money, no matter how it happens, that is on you. It's a hard lesson to learn, but nobody should work as hard as you when you're protecting *your* money.

He filed a police report, but my friend had to live with this horrible mistake while starting over to rebuild his accounts and pay down his credit card cash advances. As part of that collateral damage, his credit score took a major hit, and he was also saddled with the arduous process of rebuilding his score, which can take months and years to accomplish.

The financial toll was considerable, but even worse was the emotional toll this took on him. He didn't sleep and suffered through deep bouts of embarrassment, panic, and depression, trying to figure out how to pay his bills in the face of such a tremendous financial hit.

The story doesn't end there.

Against all odds, law enforcement tracked down the fraudster three months later. She was living across the country from my friend, and because she crossed state lines to commit fraud and other felonies, multiple agencies got involved and charged her with federal crimes. Federal charges come with much harsher penalties upon conviction.

However, proving guilt in these cases is challenging. It requires extensive forensic accounting, and limited resources often deter authorities from pursuing a full trial. As a result, plea deals are frequently made to conserve time and money, allowing white-collar criminals to face significantly reduced sentences and fines compared to the damage they've caused.

These cases can drag on for years, and even when justice is served, it often feels incomplete. Victims like my friend rarely recover any of the money they've lost, leaving a permanent financial and emotional toll.

HOW DO YOU PROTECT YOURSELF?

Fraud comes in many forms, and it's impossible to adequately cover all types of fraud you can be exposed to in a single chapter of this book. My goal is to make you aware of how easy it is to be taken, how pervasive fraud is, and how quickly it is growing worldwide.

Although I can't cover every step you can take to make yourself a harder target against fraud, you can do some general things to protect your finances from criminals. Understand that the most important thing is that it's your money, and it's up to you to do whatever you can to keep every penny you earn. Use common sense and trust your gut. If something feels bad or suspicious, stop or proceed with extreme caution.

Be aware that your banks, credit card issuers, or other financial institutions you transact with will never call, email, or text you to ask for personal information. They are more likely to freeze your account and require you to contact them to discuss any red flags.

If you get an email from an entity purporting to be an institution you do business with, don't click on links in the email unless you are sure the link is official, and you need to open it. Check the email address before you do. Sometimes, an odd-looking email is a tip-off that scammers are targeting you. Compare the email addresses with others you've gotten to see if they are similar or an exact match. A better strategy is to delete the email and call your bank or card issuer directly to address any concerns or questions they have.

If someone calls or emails you to say your bank account is compromised, hang up, check your accounts on a secure browser, and look at your accounts to ensure balances and transactions match your activity. It's also a good idea to change your passwords regularly since data breaches are becoming more widespread. New passwords make data breach information useless to thieves.

Scammers are more sophisticated, using AI communications, voice recognition, and spoofing to generate and provoke interactions with you. For example, if you get a call but don't recognize the number, don't answer it. You're not obligated to pick up the phone, although many people do. Scammers can use voice recognition to steal from you simply by capturing an innocent "Hello" or a response to "Can you hear me?" They can combine this with other public information about you to replicate a voice pattern that's impossible to discern as fake, which they use to access your accounts.

When in doubt, proceed with caution. Pause and take a beat. Think things through logically, and reach out directly to your financial partners when in doubt. They have sophisticated anti-fraud measures in place and will want to hear from you so they can share the information and look for emerging patterns or large-scale criminal activity.

COMMON TYPES OF FRAUD

Criminals are clever and constantly devise new ways to separate you from your money. In addition, fraud is prevalent and becoming worse as society places greater reliance on digital financial transactions, information, and record-keeping.

Fortunately, there are several sites you can visit to become more knowledgeable on the subject and others that can assist you if you think you've been a victim of fraud or identity theft. In addition to these resources, if you believe you are a victim of fraud, reach out to your local law enforcement agencies for immediate assistance.

- **Federal Trade Commission (FTC)—Consumer Information**
  Website: www.consumer.ftc.gov
  The FTC provides detailed information on the latest scams, how to protect yourself, and what to do if you've been scammed.

- **Better Business Bureau (BBB) Scam Tracker**
  Website: www.bbb.org/scamtracker
  BBB's Scam Tracker allows you to report and track scams and also provides warnings about current scams in your area.

- **Consumer Financial Protection Bureau (CFPB)**
  Website: www.consumerfinance.gov
  The CFPB regularly posts updates and warnings about financial scams, focusing on those affecting consumers' finances.

- **AARP Fraud Watch Network**
  Website: www.aarp.org/fraudwatchnetwork
  AARP offers a comprehensive database of fraud alerts, scam tips, and resources specifically for older adults, though it's useful for anyone.

- **National Consumers League (NCL)—Fraud.org**
  Website: www.fraud.org
  Fraud.org provides consumer alerts, reporting tools, and tips on how to avoid the latest scams.

- **IdentityTheft.gov**
  Website: www.identitytheft.gov
  This site offers resources for consumers who believe they've been victims of identity theft and provides a step-by-step recovery process.

- **FBI's Internet Crime Complaint Center (IC3)**
  Website: www.ic3.gov
  The IC3 allows users to report online fraud and scams and provides resources to protect against internet crime.

- **Social Security Administration—Fraud Prevention**
  Website: www.ssa.gov/fraud
  This site offers information on how to recognize and report Social Security-related fraud and scams.

Download the *Train Your Money Companion Guide* to access our fraud protection tools and checklists.

Scan the QR code:

CHAPTER 9
TAX STRATEGIES FOR BEGINNERS

Taxes will take a bite out of almost everything you earn over your lifetime. Although you can't avoid taxes completely, there are ways to reduce your tax burden so you can keep more of your money. The key is understanding how taxes work and learning strategies that can help minimize the impact.

Before diving into specifics, remember that this is general tax education. Everyone's financial situation is different, and it's on you to put in the work. Learn what you can and consult a tax professional so you can make smart decisions to best protect your income from unnecessary taxes.

MY FIRST TAXING EXPERIENCE

My first experience with income and taxes took place in 1995 when I was eight years old. To better understand life as an adult and be better prepared to face the world when we grew up, my parents didn't give us handouts in the form of an allowance.

Instead, we were expected to do a basic set of chores every week to contribute to the smooth running of our family home. This included making our bed, keeping our room clean, doing dishes, etc. We didn't get paid for these, but my brother Colton and I were also given the opportunity to put some spending money in our pockets by doing additional chores in addition to what was on our basic list.

We had an incentivized chore system—a list of jobs we could do to earn money—such as weeding the garden, vacuuming the house, or mopping the floors. Each chore had a dollar amount attached to it, so Colton and I always knew exactly how much we could make if we were willing to put in the work.

We could earn anywhere from $5 to $10 a week, depending on how ambitious we felt, and were paid out every Friday evening. And let me tell you, that was big money for an 8-year-old in 1995.

But my parents, being the financial gurus they are, used this as a teaching moment to introduce us to the wonderful world of taxes. Even if I managed to earn $10 in a week, I didn't get to keep all of it. Nope, just like in the real world, a portion went to taxes—our family's version of the Internal Revenue Service. For every dollar we earned, 25 percent was taken out. At the time, that money was dead and gone to me.

Yikes! You can imagine how I reacted the first time my mom took taxes out of my hard-earned chore money. I was furious. At 8 years old, I didn't have the slightest clue about taxes or why I couldn't keep everything I earned. All I knew was that it felt completely unfair. It was my first harsh lesson in the reality of money: What you make isn't always what you get to keep.

In their mission to "keep it real," my parents also had a system of fines for bad behavior—like the fines my NFL clients get for showing up late to meetings, missing practice, or breaking dress code on game day. For me, the usual offense was cussing (something I've been doing as long as I've been able to talk), and every time I got caught, it cost me. My parents would dock my pay, and while it was frustrating at the time, it was yet another tough but valuable lesson.

So, what happened to all that "tax" money we paid as kids? My mom put it into savings accounts she opened for us, which we couldn't touch until years later. That account ended up being the same one I used to build my savings when I got my first restaurant job. Wouldn't it be nice if the IRS worked that way?

By now, you've probably had your own run-ins with taxes—and trust me, there will be plenty more throughout your life. The biggest thing I learned early on is that taxes are unavoidable, but they also come with a lesson: Earning money means taking on responsibilities.

Working for money at an early age was a powerful lesson that money isn't just handed to you. You have to work for it.

You have the responsibility to not only do the work, but also making sure your money is allocated the right way. That means a portion of it will go to taxes, and another will go toward living expenses. If you're living within your means, you have the responsibility of tucking away some of your earnings to save for a rainy day.

I learned that many of my actions have financial consequences. Getting fined for cussing was one of many unforced errors. Setting aside money to deal with significant expenses such as car repairs or bigger impacts on my life is something I did right. Like me, it's up to you to figure out the potential impacts that money or a lack of money will have on your life and then act to protect yourself in a sensible way.

WHAT TO KNOW ABOUT FILING TAXES

There are countless books, podcasts, articles, and more about taxes. Some focus on minimizing your tax burden, which we'll focus on below, but others are more basic. Unless you've educated yourself on the nuts and bolts of how taxes work, you'll be at a distinct disadvantage in minimizing your burden.

Filing taxes can be fairly simple when you're just starting out, but you can still screw up your efforts if you don't learn good habits.

Here are some things you should routinely do to ensure that you will have a smoother process when you do file taxes.

- **Keep good records.** Save all financial documents (pay stubs, W-2s, receipts for deductions) and use simple apps or a filing system to organize income and expenses throughout the year.
- **Understand withholding.** As a salaried employee, employers will ask you how much of your paycheck should be set aside to make sure an appropriate amount is withheld from each paycheck. Employers withhold federal income taxes from employees' paychecks based on the information provided on Form W-4.

  Experts will tell you the goal is to create a scenario where when you file taxes, you will zero out the amount you've paid to equal the amount you owe. Filing taxes at the end of the year is a way to reconcile the taxes you owe. If you have too little withheld, you'll wind up with a tax bill at the end of the year. If you have too much withheld, you'll have a smaller paycheck, but you will set yourself up for a nice refund later.

- **Know your key tax dates.** Taxes are typically due on April 15 but may vary by a day or two if that date falls on a weekend or holiday. If you are self-employed, you must file estimated quarterly taxes throughout the year, once every quarter.
- **Adjust your withholding if your income changes.** If you get a raise, your tax situation could change. Figure out the impact and decide if you need to withhold more or less from your paycheck. Knowing that the United States has a progressive tax system is important. People with higher taxable incomes are subject to higher tax rates, while people with lower taxable incomes are subject to lower tax rates. For example, in 2024, there were seven federal income tax brackets: 10, 12, 22, 24, 32, 35, and 37 percent.
- **Don't procrastinate.** Holding off paying your taxes when they're due takes a tax situation and makes it worse. You could get hit with penalties and late charges, increasing your tax burden instead of minimizing it. Sometimes, extensions are available, but you'll still pay additional money for the privilege of extending your payments.
- **Use free and paid resources to help you file.** If you need guidance, IRS.gov has several resources that can educate you on the basics and more advanced tax issues. However, if you feel confused or if you're in over your head, be smart. Consult with a tax professional who could save you thousands of dollars by utilizing strategies to work in your favor.
- **Don't cheat!** Be aggressive but honest when filing your taxes. You will not like the outcome if you get caught bending the rules to try and save a few dollars.

HOW TO MINIMIZE YOUR TAX BURDEN

Plenty of tools and strategies exist to help you legally pay less in taxes. Let me be clear—this isn't about dodging taxes; it's about making the most of the deductions, credits, and exemptions that are already available to you.

Even if they don't apply to you right now, as your life changes, you'll find that these opportunities will come up. The key is to understand the basics now so you're ready to use them to your advantage when the time comes.

Deductions can lower your taxable income, which helps reduce how much you owe overall. Common deductions include mortgage interest, property taxes, medical expenses, charitable donations, and more.

Credits work differently—they offer a dollar-for-dollar reduction in what you owe. Some examples include credits for renewable energy investments, adoption expenses, education costs, and childcare.

Knowing the difference and how to use them can greatly affect how much of your money stays in your pocket.

Which Deduction Method is Right for You?

When you file your tax return, you'll have to decide between taking the standard deduction or itemizing your deductions. The standard deduction is a set amount you can claim without the hassle of listing every deduction you want—it's quick and easy.

Itemizing takes a bit more work because it requires gathering all the receipts and documentation for specific expenses such as medical costs, mortgage interest, or charitable donations. If your total deductions add up to more than the standard deduction, it might be worth putting in the extra effort to itemize.

Most people choose the standard deduction because it's fast and straight-forward. But if you have enough qualifying expenses, itemizing might save you more money. Either way, it's smart to keep track of your receipts and paperwork to compare both options and choose the one that works best for you.

The amount of the standard deduction depends on your filing status, and it's adjusted each year for inflation. For example:

Filing status	Standard deduction 2024	Standard deduction 2025
Single	$14,600	$15,000
Married, filing jointly	$29,200	$30,000
Married, filing separately	$14,600	$15,000
Head of household	$21,900	$22,500

What are some common retirement tax savings strategies?

The government wants you to save for retirement—it's one of the few things they actively encourage us to do! And they've set up several ways to make it happen.

Let's start with a traditional 401(k). This process lets employees contribute a portion of their wages to an individual retirement account. These contributions—called salary deferrals—are taken out before taxes, meaning they're excluded from your taxable income. On top of that, many employers sweeten the deal by matching your contributions or adding extra funds to your account as an incentive to save. The money you contribute is then invested based on your goals, with options ranging from conservative plans to more aggressive growth strategies.

Here's a simple example of how tax-deferred contributions can work in your favor: Let's say your tax rate is 25 percent. Putting $12,000 into your retirement account could save $3,000 on your current tax bill. Even better, the money you invest grows tax-free until you withdraw it in retirement—potentially at a lower tax rate if your income is less.

Another great option is an IRA (Individual Retirement Account). Like a 401(k), an IRA allows you to make tax-deferred investments as part of a larger retirement savings plan. Both options are powerful tools for building your nest egg while keeping more money in your pocket today.

There are several types of IRAs.

- A traditional IRA is a tax-advantaged personal savings plan where contributions may be tax-deductible.
- A Roth IRA is a tax-advantaged personal savings plan where contributions are not deductible, but qualified distributions may be tax-free much later. In other words, you pay taxes on the front end of your contribution but pay no taxes when you withdraw funds, including amounts you've made through investments as part of your account. The Roth IRA is one of the few tax-advantaged accounts that allows you to withdraw the money you've contributed at any time without paying taxes or penalties.
- An employer can set up a Payroll Deduction IRA plan. Employees contribute by payroll deduction to an IRA they set up with a financial institution.
- An employer sets up a Simplified Employee Pension (SEP) plan. Contributions are made by the employer directly to an IRA set up for each employee.
- A SIMPLE IRA plan is a Savings Incentive Match Plan for Employees set up by an employer. Under a SIMPLE IRA plan, employees may choose to make salary reduction contributions, and the employer makes matching or nonelective contributions.

What Are Some Other Tax-Sheltered Savings?

Although the size of allowable contributions to retirement plans is attractive to many taxpayers, there are other savings plans that also defer tax and, in some cases, help you avoid tax altogether.
- 529 education savings plans, such as prepaid tuition plans or education savings plans, are funded by after-tax dollars, but qualifying withdrawals are tax-free.
- Health coverage savings plans include health savings, medical, and flexible spending accounts (FSAs). You and/or your employer fund these plans, and contributions and withdrawals for qualifying expenses are tax-free.

- Dependent care savings accounts are similar to health flexible spending accounts but focus on helping to pay for childcare expenses while you're working. Contributions and qualifying withdrawals are tax-free.
- Invest in tax-efficient entities such as municipal bonds or index funds, which may generate lower taxable income than other investments.

Another way to reduce your tax bill is to use tax credits when possible. Refundable tax credits not only reduce your tax but can also be used to create a surplus, resulting in a refund.

- Low-income earners may qualify for the earned income tax credit, which is based on earnings, filing status, and the number of dependent children.
- The Child Tax Credit applies when you must pay for care for children or disabled dependents so that you can work or look for work. You can save up to $2,000 per qualifying child (using 2024 tax laws) if you have dependent children under 17 who meet the eligibility requirements.
- Modest earners below certain income levels may qualify for the retirement savings contributions credit. This is in addition to tax savings earned from contributions to IRAs or other retirement plans.

What Tax Records Do I Need to Keep, and for How Long?

Holding on to your tax returns and the documents you used to complete them is essential, especially if you ever get audited. Generally, the IRS has three years to decide whether they want to audit your return, so keeping your records for at least that long is a good idea. In certain cases, though, you'll want to hold onto them even longer. For instance, keep your tax records for six years if you underreported your income by more than 25 percent, seven years if you claimed a loss from a "worthless security," and indefinitely if you committed tax fraud or failed to file a return.

The U.S. tax code is huge. Thousands of pages packed with rules can leave even the most experienced tax pro scratching their head. But if you're just starting out, don't get overwhelmed. The vast majority of those regulations won't apply to you. For now, focus on the basics, and remember that being smart and efficient with handling your taxes is one of the best ways to keep more of what you earn.

CHAPTER 10
BUILDING AND WORKING WITH YOUR FINANCIAL TEAM

Do you have a go-to mechanic you trust to keep your car running smoothly? Maybe a barber or stylist who knows exactly how to make you look sharp? A doctor or dentist you wouldn't trade for anything? We all rely on experts in different areas of our lives to make things easier and better.

But here's the real question: Do you have someone you trust to protect your money and assets?

When it comes to money, there's no shortage of advice out there—literally everywhere you turn, someone has an opinion.

And that's both the best and worst thing about money advice.

Sound confusing?

Managing and protecting your money is one of the hardest and most emotional challenges you'll face, especially when starting out. You're going to have more questions than answers, more doubts than confidence, and trying to figure out what advice is solid and what's not can feel overwhelming.

That's why having your team of trusted financial pros—your Jedi money masters—isn't just helpful; it's essential. Building that team is non-negotiable if you care about your financial security, both now and in the future.

Unsurprisingly, a mountain of data supports using expert knowledge to protect and grow your assets. For example, according to one study by the National Financial Educators Council, a lack of personal finance knowledge costs the average American $1,300 a year or more. Also, in a 2019 study, Vanguard found that a hypothetical adviser-directed $500K investment would grow to over $3.4 million over 25 years, while a self-managed portfolio would total $1.69 million, a whopping 50 percent less return.

If you're just starting out, you may think you're too young or don't have enough money to warrant asking others for help and protection. Wrong! As soon as possible, you must surround yourself with the right resources to learn ways to preserve and grow your money, no matter how big or small a pile of cash and assets you have.

During dinner-table discussions with my dad, he'd often remind me that if I wasn't learning about money from the people and sources at my table, it was time to find a new table with better experts to guide me.

When you're starting out, you might be fortunate enough to have financially savvy parents (like I did) who can walk you through the basics. That works for a while, but as your income, investments, and assets grow, it's time to expand your financial team and bring in experts who can offer deeper insights.

So, who are these people, and what can they bring to the table? As you progress in life, adding the right experts to your financial team is key to staying on track.

- **Financial adviser.** Unless you study finance and investments daily and put the time in to stay abreast of market trends, products, and breaking news, you may be doing yourself a disservice by trying to keep on top of all things related to finances by yourself. Financial advisers with a fiduciary duty to put your interests above everything else are critical to protecting and preserving your assets. Finding the right one takes time. You'll need to screen several to ensure they have a good track record, understand your long- and short-term goals, and communicate with you clearly and concisely.

- **Lawyer.** Legal professionals often specialize in various parts of the financial world. Some focus on reviewing and executing contracts. Others provide tax, will, trust, and estate planning services. And others can give you business-related advice on numerous matters. Lawyers are not cheap, but compared to what you can lose by not retaining the right lawyer at the right time, they'll seem like a bargain in hindsight.

- **Accountant.** You may get by with QuickBooks or other automated software that tracks income, expenses, taxes, and other essential financial matters. Although these software packages are outstanding, there is a limit to how much they can do on a personalized basis.

If you start investing in stocks and commodities, buying real estate, running a business, or completing other more advanced financial transactions, you must have a seasoned accountant to guide you through the neverending rules and regulations. If not, you can turn your life into a miserable existence if you don't keep good records and meet deadlines.

Leveraging the knowledge of your financial team and making sure they're in sync with your goals and desires takes work. But if anything is worth investing as much time as needed to ensure you're protected, nothing trumps how you and your team manage your money.

Choose your team well as if your entire future financial health depends on it—because it does.

TIPS FOR WORKING WITH YOUR TEAM

You must decide in advance if you want to work with a smaller firm that can provide more customized and attentive service, or a more prominent firm that can offer you deeper resources and experience, but sometimes with an institutional feel or predetermined products.

As you add resources to your financial team, there is a right and wrong way to incorporate them into your personal balance sheet efforts. Here are some things to consider.

Trust But Verify

When you bring experts onto your team, you're placing a level of trust in them—that's why you asked for their help in the first place.

However, you should not go into these relationships without caution. If you hand over all responsibility and let others make all the decisions without question, you're setting yourself up for trouble. Blind trust in your finances? That's a recipe for disaster. Stay engaged, ask the right questions, and actively participate in your financial journey.

I was in a relationship for more than four years when my partner and I took a trip to Las Vegas. He was someone I trusted, and I never imagined in a million years that he would spend money the way he did. It turned out to be a very expensive lesson in trust and personal finances.

If I had been more proactive and kept a closer eye on his credit card use, I could have spared myself a lot of heartache and a lot of money. I gave someone I trusted access to my finances, but I failed to set boundaries and didn't take back control of my card before things got out of hand.

Even though I allowed him to use my card, the way he abused that privilege ultimately fell on me. It took me some time, but once the anger faded, I realized I had learned a powerful "trust but verify" lesson, one that's shaped how I approach trust and finances today.

Trust but verify can be as simple as getting receipts, checking bank account transactions, or operating in cash when combining funds as you learn your partner's financial habits. If you work with a financial adviser, be sure your financial directions are clear and concise and that your adviser executes them to your wishes.

Trust but verify also means researching your financial team *before* you retain them. Do your homework in advance. Ask lots of questions. Interview several possible advisers. If something sounds off or doesn't align with your goals, risk tolerance, and philosophy, that could be a red flag. Ask for explanations until you're satisfied, or move on to someone else.

To research and verify the qualifications of a potential financial adviser, check their credentials and licenses through the Financial Industry Regulatory Authority's (FINRA) BrokerCheck tool.

FINRA is a not-for-profit organization that regulates the securities industry in the United States. FINRA also keeps records of past disciplinary actions and complaints. Look for certifications like CFP (Certified Financial Planner), ask about a planner's experience with clients similar to you, and if they are a fiduciary who, by law, acts in your best interest.

Also, ask about their compensation structure. Are they paid based on a percentage of assets under management (AUM), hourly, or through flat fees?

Clearly define your long-term and short-term financial goals to be a better client. This will help you narrow your search to an adviser who specializes in your unique needs. Some advisers focus on things such as estate planning, tax strategies, or long-term growth, while others position themselves as generalists or have a specific niche in which they excel.

Also, find someone knowledgeable, someone you like, and someone you can connect with. Pay attention to how often and clearly they communicate. Test them by asking about things you don't fully understand, and see how well they can break down complex concepts into language that makes sense to you.

Your Circle—Your Money

Our Money Mindset chapter discussed habits, environment, and how everyone has a different relationship with money. The same is true for financial goals.

Because of my upbringing, my financial goals have always been front and center. However, you may find advisers with very strong opinions about what you should do with *your* money. There's a fine line between being a knowledgeable and strong-willed advocate and being a bully who insists on what you must do with *your* money.

The key here is that it's *your* money. You're wise to listen to the opinions of others, but in the end, you're the CEO of your finances, and financial decisions should ultimately rest with you.

Part of this goes back to trust but verify. However, the key is to accept responsibility for your money while listening to what your financial team has to say. It can be a balancing act, but ultimately, it is your circle and your money.

Right or wrong, you need to own it and your decisions.

Reframe Your Goals As Life Happens

Life is full of unexpected events, such as an unexpected $8,000 Las Vegas vacation debt or a loved one being struck by a long-term debilitating illness. Always assume catastrophic events or big changes will find you, and plan for them.

That is why having a sizable emergency fund is considered the best way to protect yourself when financial setbacks occur. If you haven't started stashing cash away yet, the time to start is now. Few things in life are worse than when you're dealt a crushing blow, and you don't have the financial resources to provide you with some level of cover.

You must remain flexible and reframe your short- and long-term goals when a job loss, health issues, a major car accident, personal injury, the death of a financial supporter, or other similar crises affect your life.

Not all life events are negative, though. If you get a big job promotion and salary bump, or if you inherit a sizable amount of money, you should also reframe your financial goals. Protect your windfall, increase your nest egg, invest a sizable portion conservatively, and practice wealth preservation with a long-term horizon in mind.

Written goals are powerful tools to keep you on track. They minimize financial disruptions, and you're more likely to hold yourself accountable when referring to a well-written and logical plan. Revisit that plan regularly and rewrite it as life events alter your finances.

Accept that life never goes exactly as you planned. Stress and worry about the unknown can be debilitating unless you have a clear road map and understand that detours will be a part of your journey.

Don't Make Critical Financial Decisions When You're Too Emotional

After my mom passed in 2013, one of my dad's mentors and a member of his financial team gave him this piece of advice.

Do not make any big financial decisions for a year.

My dad and our entire family were distraught over my mom's passing, and we were emotionally exhausted, as well as experiencing the expected levels of depression that accompany the passing of anyone you love as much as we loved my mom.

Although some decisions must be made during intense periods in your life, the more you can remove impactful decisions made in haste, the better chance you have of allowing more wisdom and perspective to influence your decision.

Anger, revenge, and irrational thinking are natural reactions to a stressful event. Even if you're usually calm and methodical, others around you might not be as equipped to handle big financial decisions in those moments.

And it's not just when someone close to you passes away. You could experience this during a job loss when you dream of moving somewhere new or fall in love and jump into living together without fully thinking through the financial details. If you come into a windfall, you might be tempted to take big risks with that "found" money. Sometimes, these decisions work out, but once the initial emotions, whether pain or euphoria, wear off, you're left facing the reality of how to move forward wisely.

As the saying goes, "common sense isn't so common." That really applies when making important discretionary financial decisions in an emotionally charged state.

If you *can* wait, you *should* wait. Allow reason and logic to guide your thoughts until intense emotions subside. You are vulnerable to making bad decisions in the heat of the moment that you could regret later. It might take a couple of days to figure things out—or weeks, months, or a year or more until a well-thought-out plan reveals itself.

YOUR SMARTEST INVESTMENT IS IN YOUR FINANCIAL LITERACY

Making money is one thing, but figuring out the smartest ways to manage it is an entirely different game.

The world is full of ethical and not-so-ethical people who are more than happy to help themselves to your hard-earned cash. And if you're not financially literate, they have a much easier time doing it.

Just as you've invested time and effort into learning how to earn money, whether through college, professional development, networking, or other opportunities, you need to invest the same energy into learning how to manage your money.

It's never too early to start. And no bank account is too small to ignore the importance of financial literacy, no matter where you're at.

The good news? Our entire world is built on the movement of wealth from employer to employee, investor to asset, etc. The more you understand how money works on all levels, the better equipped you are to make smart decisions. You're setting yourself up for long-term financial success when you do your homework.

When you make money wisdom a core part of your plan, your future becomes even more promising.

10 QUESTIONS TO ASK A FINANCIAL PROFESSIONAL

As part of your screening process, here are 10 questions to ask a financial professional before deciding on the best person to work with.

1. **What is your background and experience in financial planning?**
    This helps you understand their expertise and if it aligns with your needs.
2. **What are your areas of specialization?**
    Some advisers focus on investments, taxes, estate planning, or other niches, so knowing where their strengths lie is key.
3. **How do you get paid?**
    Understanding their compensation structure (fee-based, commission-based, or a combination) can help you assess potential conflicts of interest.
4. **How do you typically work with clients?**
    This question gives insight into their communication style, whether they offer ongoing advice or if they're more transactional.
5. **Can you provide references or testimonials from clients you've worked with?**
    Hearing from others can offer a sense of their effectiveness and professionalism.
6. **How do you help clients achieve their financial goals?**
    Learn their approach and strategies for managing money to see if they match your values and objectives.
7. **What happens if I need help outside of our scheduled meetings?**
    Knowing if they're available for advice during life's unexpected financial moments is important.
8. **How will you keep me informed about my financial situation?**
    Ask about the frequency and methods of communication to ensure they'll keep you in the loop.
9. **What's your process for making recommendations or decisions?**
    Understand how they analyze your financial situation and create strategies for you.
10. **How do you stay updated on changes in the financial industry?**
    A proactive adviser will keep up with trends and regulations, so ask how they continue their professional development.

You've come to the end of this book, but that signifies a new beginning between you and your money. We've covered several foundational topics to redefine your relationship, creating a better awareness of how money works.

The next steps are up to you.

The best thing you can do is commit to a lifelong learning process to understand how money works in your favor. Armed with the things we've covered, you're now ready to dive deeper into more advanced subjects related to investing and a long-term growth approach. Use this playbook and add your version to rack up consistent winning seasons for the rest of your life.

To accomplish this, you'll need to be disciplined and consistent. Ask questions and be curious. Dig deeper for answers that can save you thousands of dollars and put thousands of dollars in your wallet.

You must also remain flexible because as your wealth grows, your financial needs will also change. When you get married, start a family, get a big job promotion, or come into a large lump sum of money, you must be ready to adjust your goals and the approach to some parts of your finances.

Don't learn lessons the hard way like I've done a few times. Be smart and prudent to minimize the impacts of setbacks that are sure to come, like they do for everyone else.

Finally, just like athletes train their bodies and minds for peak performance, it's up to you to train your money so it creates financial peak performance for you for years to come.

ABOUT THE AUTHOR

Hillary Seiler is a Certified Financial Educator (CFE), financial expert, author, and dynamic speaker with a degree in Finance from Oregon State University and 15 years of experience delivering impactful financial education. She is the founder of Financial Footwork and the author of *Train Your Money*. Hillary works with NFL and NBA teams, businesses, and universities to help individuals train their money like a pro.

Recognized as one of the top 50 financial speakers in 2023, Hillary brings energy and authenticity to every stage she steps on. She lives in Idaho with her two Shiba Inus—Ghost and Dragon—and keeps her family, including her father and brother, at the center of her world.

To purchase bulk copies of *Train Your Money* or to book Hillary as a speaker, please email info@financialfootwork.com

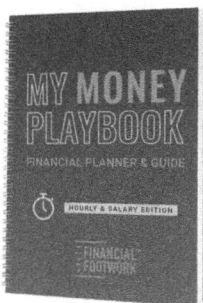

MY MONEY PLAYBOOK
HOURLY & SALARY EDITION

Self-paged financial training course with weekly exercises, coaching tips, and tools. Designed to help the user establish a strong money game.

MY MONEY PLAYBOOK
COLLEGE EDITION

Your personal financial coach for college life is more than just a planner—it's a practical easy-to-use tool built specifically for college students.

PREMIUM FINANCIAL PLANNER

Designed with simplicity, practicality, and goal achievement in mind, this 12-month planner has everything you need to transform financial habits into life-changing results.

Scan QR Code to purchase our other products.

THANK YOU FOR READING MY BOOK!

DOWNLOAD YOUR BONUS GIFT

To access your FREE copy of the *Train Your Money Companion Guide*

Scan the QR Code Here:

I appreciate your interest in my book and value your feedback
as it helps me improve future versions of this book.
I would appreciate it if you could leave your invaluable
review on Amazon.com with your feedback.
Thank you!